THE

CHICAGO

HISTORICAL

SOCIETY

1856–1956

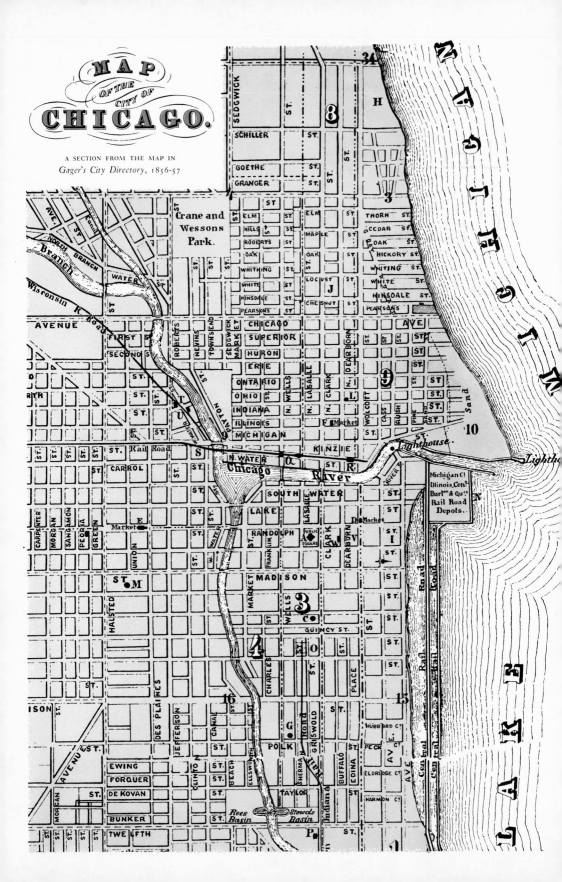

MAP OF THE CITY OF CHICAGO.

A SECTION FROM THE MAP IN
Gager's City Directory, 1856-57

THE
CHICAGO
HISTORICAL
SOCIETY

1856 – 1956

An Unconventional Chronicle

by Paul M. Angle

RAND McNALLY & COMPANY

NEW YORK • CHICAGO • SAN FRANCISCO

LIST OF

ILLUSTRATIONS

Between pages 104 *and* 105

The devastated North Side, soon after the fire of 1871.

A fire proclamation of 1871.
Samuel Stone, Assistant Librarian.

A charred hymnal, the only book in the Society's library to survive the fire.
Ruins of the Society's building, 1871.

Mrs. Henry D. Gilpin and Henry D. Gilpin.

Healy's "Honora Sneyd."
The Tremont House, Lake and Dearborn streets.

The Society's "temporary building" (1877–1892).
Fort Dearborn Memorial tablet, 1881.

John Wentworth.
Albert D. Hager, Secretary, 1877–1887.

Invitation to the Lalime meeting.
Lalime's bones.

Between pages 152 *and* 153

The Gilpin Library of the Society, 1906.
The Society's building, 1896–1932.

Fernando Jones, in Indian costume.
Invitation to the Theodore Roosevelt meeting, 1908.

Portrait of Theodore Roosevelt.

Lithographed facsimile of Lincoln's Proclamation of Emancipation, January 1, 1863.

Invitation to the Lincoln Centennial meeting, 1909.
Robert Todd Lincoln.

The Fort Dearborn Centennial exercises, 1912.
The Stephen A. Douglas Centenary exercises, 1913.

Martin F. Douglas and Miss Caroline McIlvaine
at the Douglas Centenary.

Old Settlers' meeting, October 9, 1913.
A display case of Civil War relics, about 1915.

Between pages 200 *and* 201

Charles F. Gunther.
Queen Marie of Romania arriving at the Society,
November 14, 1926.

Laying the cornerstone, July 23, 1931:
I. Newton Perry, L. Hubbard Shattuck, and
Dr. Otto L. Schmidt.
President Charles B. Pike spreads the mortar.

The new building as it looked in October, 1931.
The official opening of the new building, November 12,
1932. Charles B. Pike, Mrs. Lessing Rosenthal,
Dr. Otto L. Schmidt, George W. Dixon, Edward L.
Glaser, and Frank J. Loesch.

Princess Leilavanthi of Mysore looking at one of the
Thorne Miniature Rooms.
Sally Rand and the fans she kept.

"Gabby" Hartnett, after his famous home run.
McCutcheon exhibition: Mrs. John Lord King, John T.
McCutcheon, and Mrs. John T. McCutcheon.

Gettysburg Address Exhibit:
Governor Adlai E. Stevenson, Mayor Martin H. Kennelly,
Society President William McCormick Blair.
A fascinated youngster, Linda Reed.

Viscount Halifax and Lady Halifax, with President Joseph
M. Cudahy.
The War of 1812 Room at 6:00 p.m., November 14, 1954.

The War of 1812 Room on April 14, 1955.
A Centennial exhibit: Costumes of a century ago.

FOREWORD

❨ HISTORICAL SOCIETIES, any number of people will tell you, are stuffy organizations. In truth, many are. Yet they shouldn't be. Historical societies are concerned with history, and history is concerned with human beings, and human beings are an incredible mixture of wisdom and foolishness, bravery and cowardice, selfishness and generosity, and an infinite variety of other opposites.

A book about a historical society, therefore, should exhibit at least some of the characteristics of the stuff of history. In that conviction the Trustees of the Chicago Historical Society gave the compiler of this volume free rein, well aware of the fact that with his skill as an anthologist he combined a sense of humor and a wit sometimes sardonic. The result is exactly what we expected. Occasionally we smile a little wryly. I wish, for example, that my grandfather hadn't dismissed the Society's secretary so summarily when that worthy called to collect back dues, and I suspect that others among my colleagues and fellow members would be gratified if their forebears had behaved differently on certain occasions brought to light in these pages.

But what a small price to pay for a feature seldom found in publications of this kind: the quality of being able to laugh at one's self, or, more exactly, that degree of maturity which enables an institution to poke into its past and point with amusement as well as pride.

For there is pride in this book, and in plenty. Many of the sources which Mr. Angle uses to tell the story of a century's growth are records of high aspiration, determination, and civic dedication. The men and women who founded and nurtured the Chicago Historical Society were not small-minded people: they had a vision of a great city, and in it, an equally great cultural and educational institution. And they made the vision come true.

One must admit that a book of this kind has inherent deficiencies. It does not, cannot, tell a complete and integrated story. I know that there are important episodes in the Society's history which are not touched upon; I suspect that one or two presidents have escaped mention; and I am certain that no reference is made to several of the devoted souls who have served as secretaries, librarians, or directors.

But what the method lacks in completeness it makes up for in realism. What carefully worded narrative could convey the bitterness of defeat by fire in 1871 as vividly as the letters of William Corkran and Samuel Stone? Could anyone, years later, describe the hard road back in 1877 as convincingly as Secretary Hager did when he wrote a dead-pan account of his attempt to collect back dues? What economist's analysis could recall the shock of the market collapse in 1929 in such starkly simple fashion as dispatches written while brokers' clerks were still struggling to assess the damage of a day of chaos? Is there a humorist today who could put into *l'affaire Rand* the spontaneous gaiety of the working press of 1943?

Our centennial history may be unconventional, but we believe you will find in it as much information about the Society's past, as sure an insight into life in Chicago over the last century, and a lot more amusement than you would encounter in a book done in the orthodox manner.

HERMON DUNLAP SMITH

BIRTH

AND

CHILDHOOD

1856 – 1860

(FIVE prominent citizens of Chicago decide to form a historical society. To prove that they are in earnest, they print the invitation to the organizational meeting.

HISTORICAL SOCIETY
CHICAGO, April 2, 1856

DEAR SIR:

A Meeting of twenty or more gentlemen of this city, will be held at the Office of J. Y. Scammon, Marine Bank Building, on Thursday Evening next, at 7 1-2 o'clock, for the purpose of organizing a Historical Society. You are respectfully invited to attend.

Yours, &c.
I. N. ARNOLD,
J. D. WEBSTER,
W. BARRY,
J. H. KINZIE,
MASON BRAYMAN.

A single evening afforded too little time. The Reverend William Barry, guiding spirit of the new organization, calls the group together again.

E. B. McCAGG, ESQ.

The adjourned meeting to organise a Historical Society is to be held at Messrs. Scammon & McCagg's Rooms on

Thursday Eve at 7 1-2 o'clock.

A punctual & general attendance is desired.

W. BARRY

Chicago Apr 23 '56   by order

The effort succeeds. Notice of the result appears in the Daily Democratic Press.

CHICAGO HISTORICAL SOCIETY.—This Society has been organized by the election of the following officers:

William H. Brown, *President*

W. B. Ogden, *1st Vice President*

J. Young Scammon, *2d Vice President*

William Barry, *Recording Secretary*

C. H. Ray, *Corresponding Secretary*

Wm. Barry, *Librarian*

The interests of the Society are in the hands of the right kind of men, and we doubt not it will perform a very valuable work in rescuing and preserving the early history of the Northwest.

(*Other items of local interest appear in the same issue—April 28, 1856—of the* Democratic Press.

GOING, GONE.—The house-movers are having a busier time this spring than ever before. Scarcely a street can be found that is not blockaded day after day with locomotive domicils, departing in their old age from the bustle of business to the quiet of the suburbs. It is a fortunate thing for Chicago that bricks came into use as a building material only a few years ago, and that Athens Marble and Iron are of more recent date. Had not our first houses been built of wood it would be many years before the present palatial structures would have made their appearance.

MECHANICS' INSTITUTE.—The Institute have appointed a committee to solicit contributions for the purpose of defraying a portion of the expenses incurred in making preparations for the Mechanics' Fair, to be held in this city the first week in October. We trust the appeal will be promptly responded to by our citizens.

THANKS to McNally & Co. for New York papers of Thursday and Friday. The Knickerbocker for May, Chambers' Journal for April, and Frank Leslie's Illustrated Newspaper for May 3d, may be obtained at their counter.

CUSTOM HOUSE CONTRACT LET.—We learn that the contract for the building of the Custom House, Post Office, United States Court, etc., in our city, has been let to a gentleman from Rochester, N. Y. The occupants of the lots upon which it is to stand, corner of Monroe and Dearborn streets, have been notified to remove the present wooden buildings forthwith.

(*The Secretary and Librarian, a retired Unitarian minister from Massachusetts who had lived in Chicago for only three years, describes the founding of the Society to a friend in nearby Geneva.*

CHICAGO. April 28, 1856.

Rev. A. H. Conant,
MY DEAR BROTHER,

I write partly to apologise for my non-appearance at Geneva—owing to ill health, in part, & in part, to engrossments wh. have absorbed my time. My family left for the East, last Friday; & I have been charged also with some care & labor in starting the "Chicago Historical Society," whose laboring oar, I almost regret to say, is put into my hands. For several weeks the plan of it has been maturing with care; for you well know, that, for such an institution to be successful, & do its proper work, it must be made up of "just & impartial" men & not be perverted to the purposes of party. Fortunately we begin with men "fit & few"—some twenty—not to be enlarged beyond thirty, the first year— and never more than sixty *Resident members*. You will understand the advantage of this arrangement, in a new Society like this. We hope to make corresponding members, of whom I hope you will be one. We propose to found a Library— to establish a Depositary of Mss &c. & not least—to attempt a full and scientific exploration of aboriginal remains in the State. I think Chicago enterprise & liberality will do all this. There is already talk of buying a lot for the Society's use. Our chief men are the Ogdens, Scammons, W. H. Brown, Judges Skinner & Manierre, Drs. Blaney & Davis &c. whose names alone will inspire confidence. Do not doubt the right beginning is made. Mr. Ogden gives us rooms for the present in the 3d story of his fine building, corner of Clark & Lake Sts. & the Soc. have put upon myself their charge. . . . .

*The Rev. Mr. Barry, scouring the long-established towns of southern Illinois for historical material, slips easily into the habiliments of genteel mendicancy that men in his position wear like a **uniform**.*

ALTON. Oct. 28, 1856

Col. Stone

My DEAR SIR,

I wrote you on Sunday supposing I should leave here today; but I shall not leave till tomorrow, & *may* be detained till Thursday morn before starting for the South. I still continue my collections having today been favored with large contributions of newspaper files, valuable periodicals & tracts—as well as public documents furnished by Maj. Hunter, formerly of the U. S. Service. It is my intention to forward perhaps three boxes to you by Express. Could you not induce the Express Agent at Chicago, to make some abatement in the charge of carriage in consideration of the object?

If not inconvenient to you, would you please call at the office, and state to them the nature & character of our Society's labors—that we are all volunteers giving our service to this work for the public good & that, while our expenses are considerable, our means are limited. If it would be consistent & agreeable to them to make any abatement of their usual charges for the benefit of the Society, it will be appreciated by the members, and be received as their contribution to the work itself. . . . .

Meeting on December 18, 1856, the young Society adopts a seal.

. . . . The legal seal of the Society, executed in Chicago, was accepted. It bears the Society's name, "Soc Historic Chicago," above the shield, on the superior part of which is the design of a wigwam on the lake shore, near the latter a

ship under sail with the rising sun; on the inferior an open
book. The shield is nearly encircled by a scroll with the
motto, "Monumenta Histor Conser." Beneath is the date of
the Society's institution, 1856. . . . .

(*In his capacity as a member of the Illinios House of Representatives, Isaac N. Arnold, founder-member of the Chicago
Historical Society, starts an act of incorporation through the
legislature. The* House Journal *for January 7, 1857, has this
record:*

. . . . Mr. Arnold, on leave, introduced a bill for "An
act to incorporate the Chicago Historical Society"; which
was read a first time, and ordered to second reading.

On motion of Mr. Arnold, the rule was suspended, the
bill read a second time, by its title, and referred to the committee on banks and corporations. . . . .

*The House passes the bill on January 21 by a vote of 50
to 0, the Senate, on February 6, by a vote of 21 to 1. The lone*

dissenter, moved by reasons lost in the mists of time, is Samuel H. Martin of the counties of Williamson, Saline, White, Hamilton, and Franklin. The Governor affixes his signature on February 7. To this day, the act serves as the Society's basic charter. The text, with some omissions, follows.

AN ACT TO INCORPORATE THE CHICAGO HISTORICAL SOCIETY

WHEREAS, It is conducive to the public good of a state to encourage such institutions as have for their object to collect and preserve the memorials of its founders and benefactors, as well as the historical evidences of its progress in settlement and population, and in the arts, improvements and institutions which distinguish a civilized community, to transmit the same for the instruction and benefit of future generations—

Section 1. *Be it enacted by the people of the state of Illinois, represented in the General Assembly,* That William H. Brown, William B. Ogden, J. Young Scammon, Mason Brayman, Mark Skinner, George Manierre, John H. Kinzie, J. V. Z. Blaney, E. J. Tinkham, J. D. Webster, W. A. Smallwood, V. H. Higgins, N. S. Davis, Charles H. Ray, S. D. Ward, M. D. Ogden, F. Scammon, E. B. McCagg, and William Barry, all of the city of Chicago, who have associated for the purposes aforesaid, be and are hereby formed into and constituted a body politic and corporate, by the name of the "Chicago Historical Society"; and that they and their successors, and such others as shall be legally elected by them as their associates, shall be and continue a body politic and corporate, by that name, forever.

2. Said society shall have power to elect a president

and all necessary officers, and shall have one common seal. . . . .

3. The said society shall have power to make all orders and by-laws for governing its members and property, not repugnant to the laws of this state. . . . .

4. The said society may, from time to time, establish rules for electing officers and members, and also times and places for holding meetings. . . . .

5. The said society shall have power to elect corresponding and honorary members thereof, in the various parts of this state, and of the several United States, and also in foreign countries, at their discretion: *Provided, however,* that the number of resident members of said society shall never exceed sixty*. . . . .

6. Members of the legislature of this state, in either branch, and judges of the supreme court, and officers of state shall and may have free access to the Society's library and cabinet. . . . .

❨ *The Chicago Historical Society holds its first annual meeting at the home of its President, William H. Brown, on June 9, 1857. Before "a considerable number of ladies and gentlemen, invited guests of the Society," Mr. Brown reads a memoir of Daniel Pope Cook, the Illinois Congressman for whom Cook County was named, and then asks the Rev. Mr. Barry to present his report as Librarian. Excerpts follow.*

. . . . The Chicago Historical Society had its origin in a prevailing and long-cherished belief that this was an ap-

---

* *This limitation was removed by an Act of the legislature approved January 30, 1867.*

propriate point for a State Institution of a comprehensive, efficient, and desirable character. Itself, a populous commercial metropolis of near 100,000 souls, the probable center of trade hereafter for the vast region of the North West, with all points of which it is being connected by numerous radiating avenues, possessing too, in as full measures as could be expected, the resources pecuniary and intellectual, desirable for such an institution, no point could be more favorable for a depository of historical materials, the institution of an extensive documentary Library, and the prosecution of historical research, and the diffusion of historical information. . . . .

It is proper to observe, that the Society commenced its existence without any particular appeal to the public patronage, or the favoring influence of a popular excitement. This was done in the belief that an unostentatious, compact, and harmonious organization (although involving heavier burdens on its members) would prove more effective in its operations, as well as satisfactory in its results, and that the confidence and support of the public could be relied upon, so far as its operations and results should substantially meet them. . . . .

The success of the Society's operations the past year through the natural difficulties incident to a new organization, while in part attributable to the generous aid it has received abroad, especially from the cities of Boston and Worcester in Massachusetts, from Providence in Rhode Island, and from the City of Philadelphia, has also been greatly promoted by the liberal pecuniary aid received from the City of Chicago, as will appear from the Treasurer's Report, more than $600 having been received during the year (the greater part from members) in donations in addition to the amount contributed by members under the Society's bylaws. Such expressions of encouraging interest in the Society's labors are warmly appreciated, and it is hoped that it may continue to merit the well-known bounty of the public, upon which it must depend for an early and full realization of its objects of public good.

So extensive have now become its collections and operations, that the first and most pressing want is now an adequate provision to secure the permanent services of a competent person of ability and experience to undertake the principal labor required for its successful management in the place of the individual who has hitherto directed it, as well as to ensure the possession by purchase from year to year of such works of value and necessity to us, as may be required by the library. . . . .

The aggregate collection in the Society's library as enumerated in the Book of Donations is:

Total no. of bound volumes and yearly
files of newspapers and periodicals   3,577
Total no. of unbound public documents,
reports of institutions, political, religious,
and scientific pamphlets, broadsides   4,966
Total no. of charts in bound volumes or
single sheets   101

In the above, manuscripts collected by the Society, and considerable in number, are not included. An exact enumeration would probably furnish a grand total of about 9,000.

WILLIAM BARRY

❨ William H. Bissell, veteran of the Mexican War, friend of Abraham Lincoln, and first Republican Governor of Illinois, notices the Society in his annual message to the General Assembly, January 3, 1859.

. . . . For a reason, presently to be stated, I desire to direct your attention to the Chicago Historical Society. Although of a comparatively brief existence, it has already attracted the attention of reading and scientific men throughout the state. Possessing a library of over 16,000 volumes, and making constant accessions of rare and valuable books, it promises, at no distant day, to surpass in capacity for usefulness any other society of the kind in the west.

Already it has rendered especial service, by rescuing from oblivion much of the early history of Illinois, and preserving a detailed account of passing events, which are to become history by and by. As a means of increasing its capacity for good and extending its sphere of usefulness, I respectfully recommend that a law be passed directing the secretary of state, after the close of each session of the legislature, to furnish to that society one hundred copies each of all the public documents ordered to be printed by either house, to be used by it in making exchanges with other societies, and with states. . . . . I can hardly conceive of any other plan on which a trivial appropriation can be made to contribute so extensively to the general good. . . . .

❨ On January 29, 1860, Henry D. Gilpin died in Philadelphia, where he had resided since his birth in 1801. Beginning life as a lawyer, and becoming eminent enough in his profession to serve as Attorney General of the United States,

Gilpin had devoted his later years to literary and cultural pursuits, had written and edited several historical treatises, and had assembled one of the largest private libraries in the country. The significance of his death to the Chicago Historical Society comes out in the minutes of a Society meeting held on February 21, 1860.

. . . . A letter [was read] addressed to the President from Charles McAllister of Philadelphia, one of the executors of the last will and testament of the late Hon. Henry D. Gilpin, of that city, deceased, and communicating the intelligence that this Society has been declared one of the residuary legatees in the provision of said will; and a printed copy of the will was transmitted for the Society's information and use.

The Hon. William B. Ogden then submitted some extended and impressive remarks upon the personal character of the late Mr. Gilpin, with whom he had been long acquainted; upon his fine culture and scholarly tastes; the rare beauty and harmony of his domestic relations; the refined grace and unostentatious hospitalities of his household; the judgment, taste, and liberality with which he surrounded himself with the choicest treasures of literature, and many beautiful works of art; and the spontaneous munificence he has displayed in the important bequests he had provided (with others) for this Society, as an evidence of the warm personal interest felt by him in the prosperity and welfare of, this city, in which he had, for many years, possessed extensive landed interests. . . . .

The will of Henry D. Gilpin provided for a life estate to his mother and Mrs. Gilpin, and directed the survivor, or

the executors after the death of the survivor, to make specific
bequests totaling $100,000 to a number of relatives. The resid-
uary estate was then to be divided equally between the
Pennsylvania Academy of the Fine Arts, the Historical So-
ciety of Pennsylvania, and the Chicago Historical Society.

It is doubtful if the members attending the meeting of
February 21, 1860, and listening with gratification to the
reading of the following passage, caught the ominous signifi-
cance of two dates: the will was made on January 17, 1860;
Gilpin died on January 29. Pennsylvania law provided that
bequests to charitable, educational, and religious organiza-
tions were void if the testator died within thirty days.

. . . . The remaining third part of the said rest and
residue of my estate, real and personal to the President and
eldest Vice-president or Director of the Historical Society
of Chicago for the time being and to Richard A. Gilpin,
Henry D. Gilpin junior and Charles Macalester of Philadelphia and William B. Ogden of Chicago and the survivor
and survivors of them in trust to invest and re-invest the
same at interest in the public stocks of the City of Chicago
and after a period of ten years (and as much longer as they
may deem expedient) then to appropriate the income accumulated up to that time by such investment and re-
investment to the erection by themselves or in such manner
and plan as they shall approve of a fire-proof Library building
to be a part of a fire-proof edifice of the said Society, when
one shall be erected, but to be in itself fire-proof entirely
distinct from any other portion of the said edifice though
connected with and forming a part of it and to be designated
"The Gilpin Library of the Historical Society of Chicago."

After the said edifice and building shall be entirely completed then I direct the said last named Trustees and their successors to appropriate annually to the use of the said Gilpin Library the entire income of the said last mentioned third part of the said rest and residue of my estate real and personal and to continue to invest and re-invest the principal of the same in the public stocks last mentioned. I authorize the said last named Trustees and their successors to appropriate annually to the use of the said last mentioned Gilpin Library the entire income of the said one-third part of the said rest and residue of my estate and to continue to invest and re-invest the principal of the same in the public stocks aforesaid. I authorize the said last named Trustees and their successors to make all rules and regulations for the establishment and conduct of the said Library co-operating with and having the assent of the said Historical Society; but I direct that none of the books or other articles be taken therefrom, but that the same be used (with liberal arrangements) by Students at the Library. . . . .

❰ Chicago, engrossed in the presidential campaign of 1860, suddenly wakes up to the fact that within a few days the city will be host to the Prince of Wales, traveling as Baron Renfrew, and his suite. The Historical Society prepares for the event.

. . . . The anticipated visit to the city of a company of distinguished personages from Great Britain having called forth some remarks, the Society instructed the secretary to cause to be presented to His Grace the Duke of Newcastle, colonial secretary of Great Britain, with appropriate gratulatory expression such documents etc., relating to the city and the Northwest, in their possession for such disposal as may illustrate the history, resources, commerce etc. of this region. . . . .

The royal party visits the Society's rooms, now located in the Newberry Building, Wells and Kinzie streets. Mr. Barry records the event in his diary.

Saturday, Sept. 22nd, 1860. At noon, while writing a letter, the Mayor (John Wentworth) entered, accompanied by the Prince of Wales and suite, who were introduced by the Mayor, and inspected our rooms. The Duke of Newcastle engaged my attention, and Col. Stone accompanied the Prince. The Duke expressed pleasure at his election as an Honorary Member, promising his valuable aid in documents, and will write answer tomorrow.

The party were much interested in Jo Smith's "Times and Seasons," one of the party desiring to obtain a copy.

The Prince and suite left their autographs.

(*The Society receives some publicity that must have made the Rev. Mr. Barry wince. I. H. Burch, a wealthy Chicago banker residing at Naperville, sues his wife for divorce, alleging criminal relations with David Stuart. In the trial of the case in November, 1860, a meeting of the Chicago Historical Society figures importantly. Witness the deposition of Joseph D. Long.*

Mr. Caulfield, for the defence, then read the deposition of J. D. Long, lawyer. The witness testified—

I am acquainted with Isaac H. Burch a year and a half

or two years. I have seen him in the office of Stuart & Ayer. I have known David Stuart two years. I recollect the meeting of the Chicago Historical Society in the fall or winter of 1859 or 1860; the meeting was held in the fall of 1859, or 1859 or 1860, in the night time. I was at the house of David Stuart.* Mr. Stuart and his wife and others were present; we were engaged in various occupations from half-past six to seven. I was then leaving the house, and went with Walter L. Peck to call upon the Misses Barry, who lived a mile distant; I left Stuart lying on a sofa a little before seven o'clock; and after leaving with Walter Peck I remarked to him that it would be doubtful if we would meet the Misses Barry at home, as they would be likely to be at the meeting of the Historical Society at Brown's; we did not find the Misses Barry home; I asked the woman who came to the door if the young ladies were at home; I asked or suggested whether they were at the Historical Society; I am certain from the reply that Mr. Barry and his wife were gone to the Historical Society; I do not recollect the exact conversation that took place; we got back to Mr. Stuart's about half-past seven or eight; Mr. Stuart was lying on the sofa; myself and Mr. Peck stayed until ten o'clock playing euchre with Mr. Stuart and Mr. Burrill; when I first saw Mr. Stuart, on my return to his house, I told him that we found the Misses Barry had gone to the Historical Society; I was living at Mr. Stuart's at that time; I can only approximate to the date; I heard that it was made a point in this case that Stuart was at Mr. Burch's house on the evening of the meeting of

---

* *This was one of the occasions when Stuart was alleged to have attempted criminal intercourse with Mrs. Burch.*

the Historical Society at Mr. Brown's; and then I remembered
the circumstances of calling on the Misses Barry.

*Mr. Barry also recalled the meeting of the Society. The
record continues:*

Mr. Beckwith read the deposition of Wm. Barry:

I know the parties to this suit about three years; am the
secretary of the Chicago Historical Society since its first
organization, April 24th, 1856; the meeting of the Historical
Society was held at Mr. W. H. Brown's house, November 29th, 1859, on Tuesday evening; I think the members
were notified to assemble about 7—it broke up about 10
o'clock—shortly after.

*Orville H. Browning, one of Mrs. Burch's counsel, re-
cords the outcome of the case in his diary.*

Monday Decr. 10. About 5 inches of snow this morning
but thawing through the day. Court met at 9 A.M. At 10
Mr Van Arman resumed his argument, and concluded at 1¼.
Court then adjourned till 2½, at which time the Judge charged
the jury, and they retired at 3½. At 5½ it was announced the
jury had agreed—we went to the Court house, and received
a verdict for the Defendant amid the wildest excitement. The
lawyers in the defence, and a large crowd of citizens and
the jury went to call on Mrs Burch, and Mrs Turner her
mother. Mrs Turner threw her arms around my neck, kissed
me and wept like a child. At night the citizens with a band
of music came and serenaded me, and I had to make them a
little speech. The jury all called on me at my room, and

afterwards Gil Davidson, and some of his friends made me go over to the preemption house* and drink and rejoice with them until 11 o'clock. It was a wonderful triumph, and the approval of the verdict seems to be unanimous.

⟨ *The Society confers its highest honor on the most prominent citizen of the state. (Lincoln's letter of acceptance was destroyed when all Society records prior to 1871 were burned.)*

CHICAGO HISTORICAL SOCIETY
Historical Rooms
Jan. 18, 1861.

To the Hon. Abraham Lincoln.
DEAR SIR,

I have the honor to inform you, that, at a statute meeting of this Society, held the 15th instant, you were elected one of its Honorary members.

Will you please oblige the Society, by informing the Secretary in writing, if it is agreeable to you to accept this appointment.

I have the honor to be,
with the highest respect,
Dear Sir,
Your obedient servant,
WILLIAM BARRY,
Secy. &c.

---

* *The Preemption House, Naperville's principal hotel and one of the oldest taverns in the state, even in 1860.*

YOUTH

1860 – 1871

(*AS the Civil War nears its end the Society stirs with ambition. Its rooms are stuffed with the accumulations of its indefatigable librarian, and it must have space if it is not to be choked to death. A building of its own is the solution. At the annual meeting in November, 1864, the members make the decision, appoint a Building Committee, and appeal to the people of a growing, thriving city for funds. The Building Committee loses no time. On January 31, 1865, it makes its first report.*

The Building Committee, Messrs. G. F. Rumsey, E. B. McCagg, and E. H. Sheldon, reported that they had increased the building fund to $30,400, and had purchased of Hon. I. N. Arnold the lot on the northwest corner of Ontario and Dearborn, 120 x 131, at a cost of $18,000 less $2,000, the amount of Mr. Arnold's subscription, which sum they had paid, and received a deed therefor. There now remains $13,000 in the hands of the committee to be applied towards the erection of a suitable building. The committee presented a plan for the same which had received their unanimous approval, and which they recommended for adoption provided it is thought sufficient funds can be obtained to carry it out.

The plan contemplates the erection of the west 42 feet front of the main building by 80 feet deep, which will be complete in itself, and answer all the requirements of the Society for several years to come, and at the same time form a part of the main building when completed. It is proposed to form the first floor of brick, with arches sprung from brick columns in the basement, and the floor of the library room with brick arches sprung from wrought iron girders. To build in this manner with cut stone front it is estimated the building will cost from $30,000 to $35,000. There have been some promises made so that the committee think that it is safe to say the sum of $15,000 is provided for, and they are of the opinion that if they have the hearty coöperation of the members of the Society, a sufficient amount can be obtained to carry out this plan, provided it should meet their approval.

The building may be cheapened very materially by substituting wooden floors, and making the front of brick, to replace it with stone in the future.

Some discussion ensued on the report, and the expression of the members was unanimously against wooden floors, and in favor of making every detail of the building solid, substantial, and fireproof.

The plan proposed by the committee comprises spacious rooms on the first floor for the various offices of the Society, including a handsome lecture room, etc.

The entire second floor is to be devoted to the library, with proper appliances for its care. The outside of the building will present a beautiful and imposing appearance, and the *tout ensemble* will be creditable alike to the Society and the city.

On motion of Judge Skinner the plan proposed by the committee was unanimously adopted, and it was resolved to push the work along with energy, and if possible complete the building the coming season.

❲ *In June, 1866, the Rev. William Barry, mainstay of the Society during its first decade, resigns as Secretary and Librarian because of ill health. At the Society's next meeting, held in July, those present take a critical look at the "exclusive" policy upon which Mr. Barry had insisted. The minutes of the meeting record their ruminations.*

. . . . An informal discussion then took place, as to the manner in which the Society should deport itself to the public in the future. It was freely conceded that the Society would be more successful if it afforded to the public greater facilities in obtaining information. At the same time, it was stated that any other course than the apparently exclusive one hitherto pursued, has been simply impossible in the cramped condition of things, in the present rooms, which forbids even an arrangement of the books in the library, to say nothing of extensive reference. It was agreed that the attempt to unchaotize the mass was useless, previous to the change of location, but that so soon as the new building was fitted for the reception of the treasures now in the possession of the Society, the treasures shall be properly classified and arranged for reference and rooms set apart for the reading of the public.

❲ *With its new building nearing completion, the Society decides that it needs a young, energetic, trained librarian. Their choice falls on William Corkran, of New York City, whose qualifications include a flair for acute observation and acidulous expression. Mr. Corkran arrives in Chicago in March, 1868. He is not pleased with what he sees.*

. . . . To a person who had lived for years in any great city, his first impressions of Chicago were anything but agreeable.

As the train slowly entered the city at the Pittsburgh and Fort Wayne Depot, surrounded on all sides by low, dirty-looking shanties, around which were gathered numerous dirty-looking men and women, while still dirtier children played in the black muddy streets, where hogs, cows, chickens and geese were wallowing, they presented a sight not calculated to produce the most favorable impressions upon one who had been allured to its shores by the promises held out of finding himself in the Garden City of the West. Now the train gradually slackens, the bell ringing its sharp warning, passing between houses and fences on which were invariably painted in white letters, "Doctor Clarke's itch ointment." Add to these a now thick hazy smoky atmosphere, a chilling blast from the lake, and a most horrible smell from the river, and you have at last arrived in the centre of that great city of Chicago.

How strange everything seemed to us on our arrival. First, the houses were low, in many instances utterly filthy, whilst the small stores that ran directly down Madison Street east to Wells, and from Wells north and south, were of a class resembling the dirtiest booths of the poor Greeks in the lowest parts of Athens, Hounds Ditch of London, the Quartier du Temple of Paris, or the Five Points of New York— and yet these were the principal streets of Chicago, principal in this, that here was a great part of the business done, of that class of cheap clothing, cheap saloons, cheap boarding houses, in fact cheap everything, where many a poor fellow has to go, not only on his first arrival but all the while he remained in Chicago. These streets extended for miles, and every one of them presented the same appearance. We could not help shuddering as we looked on these low, ricketty shells, built of dry timber, at the possible horrors attendant a conflagration. Pursuing our way down Wells Street we soon reached the office of the Board of Public Works, which were situated near the bridge in a large ugly building of peculiar architecture.

As we had a letter to one of the principal men, we were ushered into his office and stood face to face with a representative of the West. As he perused our letter we took him in at a glance. Here he is:

A tall, lanky, dried-up old gentleman, dressed in the coarsest garb, his lips almost black from tobacco juice, whilst one side of his cheek was swollen from the much cherished quid. There was a look about him which did not impress us very favorably; it was a close, hard, ill-tempered look, as if he could not say a kind word. Soon he had finished the perusal of our letter, glared at us through his spectacles, then stooping over he expectorated a small Niagara of tobacco juice, which almost made us sick, and asked how long we had been in Chicago.

"Just arrived."

"Then how did you find your way here?"

"We had very little difficulty, having studied the map and found we had to cross from West Madison Street bridge to Wells Street, and here we are."

"Chicago is a great place, Sir! I understand you are going to settle down here—in the Historical Society, I believe? Well, I hope you'll like it. In the meantime I will introduce you to Mr. McCagg, the corresponding secretary, who invited you out here."

Following our worthy pioneer, we entered a peculiar looking waggon he called his buggy, which resembled the cover of a dry goods box on wheels. Driving slowly down Lake Street, which was then the principal street, he pointed out some three or four stores, which he assured me were unequalled in the East for grandeur, business, or wealth. We could not help an involuntary smile at the impertinence of the assertion, as we believed we could find as good stores on Tenth, or even Eleventh Avenue, New York.

Having driven the length of a couple of blocks, we arrived at the Marine Bank Building, where Mr. McCagg's office was, and were requested to note the beauty of the architecture of this very peculiar building, which in fact was nothing but a big square stone block, with no very great beauty about it. We found Mr. McCagg in his sanctum, conversing with a gentleman on legal matters. Mr. McCagg was a slight active middle-sized man who spoke and moved very quick, and we were assured was one of the representative men of the West.

After being introduced, we were again assured that Chicago was a great place, and apologies made for its being still young, and were then accompanied to the rooms of the Historical Society, and at last left to our own devices to find suitable accommodations.

The city of Chicago was laid out in three great divisions or Sides. These were the North Side, South Side, and West Side, so-called from their being divided by the Chicago River, a dirty narrow stream emitting an effluvium that would have puzzled any scientist to analyze. We were assured however that this vast sink of black greasy waters was not unhealthy and that we would soon become so accustomed to it as not to mind it at all.

To a new arrival, a walk through the streets of Chicago was anything but agreeable. So long as he kept in the great thoroughfares it was well enough, but if it was necessary to go through any of the side streets, then began a system of clambering up and down six or seven steep little steps, or running down a plank and up another. This system was called grading or levelling, or in other words, when you stood below, you stood just two feet above the original level of Chicago, but when above, the proper level of six feet.

The main thoroughfares such as North and South Clark Street, which was the vertebra of Chicago running from one end to the other of the city, and changing name as it was separated by the river, was a broad street whose wooden pavement, when not broken, was pleasant to drive on. As we faced north, we were not at all prepossessed by the number of miserable low wooden stores, with here and there a taller building standing frowningly looking down upon its surroundings, presenting a huge pile of ugly bricks, which seemed in some cases as if they could be blown down by a gale.

The North Side of the city was a curious melange of wealth and extreme poverty, the residences of the wealthy being on the east side of Clark Street, whilst the miserable low dirty shanties of the poor were immediately west. North Clark Street was a long, broad street paved with wood, having a car track in the middle, whilst its wooden sidewalks now and then half rotten and mostly roughened through wear, were anything but pleasant to walk on, as the foot would strike against a nail which had sprung from the planking. The stores on either side of the street were mostly low wooden houses, whose fronts were anything but prepossessing, whilst their rears were utterly miserable. This street was the great centre for lager beer saloons, Turner Halls, concert rooms, small groceries, drug stores, and numerous other stores, kept mostly by Germans, of which Jews predominated. It was a thorough Western street in every sense of the words, for here were found numerous small dealers in every branch of trade, running a business on small capital, sleeping and living in the rear of their stores, whilst the upper floor was rented to boarders and lodgers, and as prices were generally as high as in the first stores of the city, it is no wonder that a great number of these people succeeded soon in buying up a house and lot of their own, and becoming property owners.

Among the wealthy residents of Chicago, who live on this side of the city, were those known as the old families, or first residents. Of these the most prominent were the Hubbards, Ogdens, Sheldons, McCaggs, Rumseys, and Arnolds, who owned not only beautiful residences surrounded by large gardens and hot houses, but in many instances one or two whole blocks of houses which they rented at exorbitant prices.

In summer the North Side was by far the prettiest part of the city, with its numerous large gardens filled with the choicest flowers, its old trees grown to enormous size throwing their leafy shadows across street and sidewalk, presenting in many instances a perfect bower.

As you walked by Mr. Ogden's beautiful place, with its choice flowers planted in numerous beds, and its beautiful croquet lawn so soft and fresh, and then crossed to Mr. Walter Newberry's magnificent residence, surrounded also by a beautiful garden, orchard, and lawn, whilst on the opposite side of the street stood Mr. Arnold's large house, situated in the midst of a perfect sea of flowers, then add to these the perfect stillness of the place, disturbed only by the occasional passing of an elegant turnout, or the low murmur of the lake,

upon whose deep blue bosom sailed numerous jaunty vessels
with their snow-white sails spread out to catch the slightest
breath of heaven, laden with the wealth and produce of the
West—then it was, that indeed poor Chicago presented the
appearance of a real garden city. At such times the very nature
of the people seemed changed, there was a seeming thawing-
out of their natural coldness and harshness, and as you passed
by some of these old residents, they either welcomed you in a
kinder manner, or seemed as if even they were impressed by
the beauty of the surroundings. . . . .

([*By the fall of 1868 the new building is ready for occupancy.
Invitations go out for a gala opening meeting on the evening
of November 19. The next day the* Tribune *carries the story.*

The Chicago Historical Society, which has now passed into
the 3d lustrum of its existence, formally celebrated last night,
the inauguration of its new building at the corner of Dearborn and Ontario streets.

The building when fully completed in accordance with
the plan of Burling & Co. will have a frontage of 120 on
Ontario by 132 on Dearborn. . . . . There will be a court or
open space in the center of the building extending from the
first floor to the top, and will be covered by a glass roof. The
court will be . . . . finished with smooth walls and a marble
floor, and it is intended for the exhibition of statuary and
works of art. . . . . The 2nd story . . . . will be used ex-
clusively for the library and will be lighted by large skylights.
The principal entrances will be on Ontario St. Thus much for
the plans.

There has been erected thus far only the west part of

the building, fronting 42 feet on Ontario Street and running back 39 feet, which will for some years accommodate the Society and its accumulated stock of books. The building is fireproof, with floors of iron beams and a brick arch finished with marble tiling, and a metal roof with a frame work of iron. The second floor has been fitted up with shelving, and affords space for the books on hand.

Every preparation had been made to enhance the pleasure of so interesting an occasion. The office on the 1st floor was brilliantly lit up, and served as a reception room where the numerous visitors were received by the urbane secretary. From this impromptu cloak room, all passed up the flight of stairs to the library, which was brilliantly illuminated. The walls covered with bookcases and adorned with portraits added greatly to the charm of the scene. Several of the prominent citizens of Chicago, among them Capt. Turner, Thomas Hoyne, Lt. Gov. Bross, Elliott Anthony, Geo. L. Dunlap, Dr. J. H. Rauch, Walter Kimball, Dr. J. H. Foster, E. J. Tinkham, Col. Hammond, B. W. Raymond, E. H. Sheldon, J. H. Dunham, Samuel W. Fuller, Wm. H. Bradley, Wm. E. Doggett were present. . . . .

The newspaper account made no mention of an event which threw the shadow of sadness over those who gathered in the new building: the receipt of word, that very day, that Walter L. Newberry, the Society's President, had died while on his way to Europe. The uncertainty of life is uppermost in the mind of J. Young Scammon as he opens the meeting.

Ladies and Gentlemen: The Chicago Historical Society gratefully rejoices in being able to exhibit to you this fine building, and so much of a great public library. It is only a few years since some gentlemen met together in the upper story of a building on La Salle Street, when there was scarcely a business house south of us—the one where we met being between Lake and Randolph streets. They were a few people who were desirous of doing something to found a public library for the City of Chicago. The leading mind, then, was the Rev. William Barry, our first Secretary and Treasurer, who is now in Europe. From that movement has resulted this fine edifice, and so much of the great public library as we now possess.

I am reminded by the fact that, at the last meeting of the Society which I had the pleasure of attending, the death of Mr. William H. Brown, our first President, was announced, and that, on this day, the removal to the spiritual world of the last President who has ever presided over this institution, has been made known through the public press—of the transitory character of individual life. Such events should deeply impress upon the minds of all the necessity that those of us who desire to administer upon our own estates, or labor for this and similar institutions, while we have anything to work with, should at once take hold and do something to endow the public institutions—the great charities which we owe to the City of Chicago and to the State of Illinois, which have made us what we are.

I do not admit that any man who endows the Chicago Historical Society, the University of Chicago, the Academy of Sciences, the Chicago Astronomical Society, or any other of our public institutions, is a *mere donor* to the public good. Every man who has made his fortune, or found his home, his prosperity, or his happiness in this land, owes it to the public, owes it to Chicago, owes it to the State of Illinois, owes it to his duty and his God, to see that those institutions, which it is our duty now to found, are placed upon a solid basis. . . . .

It is not my desire to address you at any length on this occasion. One of our oldest and most distinguished members has consented to perform this office. It remains for me only to bid you a hearty welcome to our rooms and library, while I request each and all who are present to do the Society the honor to subscribe their names in our Autograph Book, which now lies upon the table before me. I have the honor to introduce to you the Hon. Isaac N. Arnold. . . . .

The man who rises to address the Society is one of Chicago's outstanding citizens—successful lawyer, antislavery leader, former member of the state legislature and the national House of Representatives, and, only two years previously, author of The History of Abraham Lincoln and the Overthrow of Slavery. *He speaks the convictions of a man of culture.*

. . . . The position of Chicago, as the metropolitan city of the Northwest, is, I suppose, fixed. Its vast railroad system, its lake commerce through New York and by the St. Lawrence to the ocean, its connection, by canal, with the great central river of the continent; already the great depot of the staples of an agricultural district continental in its extent; the centre of the products of the forest, the mines, and the fields of the great central regions of the Republic; soon, by means of the Pacific Railroad, to be the great distributor of the products of the old Asiatic world, as it now is of the new, it must of necessity be the great city of the interior, perhaps of the nation.

If Chicago, already so eminent in many things, aspires to become also a literary centre, and to irradiate the great valley of which she is the commercial representative, she must foster with liberal aid and generous appreciation her literary institutions; more, she must encourage and honor men of culture, letters, and science.

Her merchant princes must learn that while it is something to build an elevator, to make a harbor, to open a canal, to construct a railroad, it is also something equally honorable, at least, to found a library, to establish a college, a university, or a school of learning.

No one doubts that our citizens have the bold enterprise, the sleepless activity, the earnestness, and energy which will enable them to make the most of their material advantages, but no wise citizen will be satisfied with this. It is time for Chicago to aim at a generous emulation with her sisters in the arts, in taste, in letters, in all those pursuits which give grace, elevation, and dignity to the human intellect and character.

Chicago must not follow Carthage, or Venice, or Liverpool, or Amsterdam, alone, as models; let her learn, also, from Alexandria, Athens, and Florence. . . . .

We have boasted long enough of our grain-elevators, our railroads, our trade in wheat and lumber, our business palaces; let us now have libraries, galleries of art, scientific museums, noble architecture, and public parks, specimens of landscape gardening, and a local literature; otherwise there is danger that Chicago will become merely a place where ambitious young men will come to make money and achieve a fortune, and then go elsewhere to enjoy it. You must have culture, taste, beauty, art, literature, or there is danger that our city will become a town of mere traders and money-getters; rude, unlettered, hard, sharp, and grasping. Let us sow the seed generously, and even if we do not ourselves live to gather the fruit, those who shall hereafter reap the harvest will bless the sowers. . . . .

Today it needs no prophecy to see that the "Star of Empire" will rest upon the great valley of the Mississippi. Here in this great central region of the Republic, *is to be*—perhaps, since the close of the great rebellion, it is not too much to say, *is already*—the seat of empire. It is a truth, which the world is learning to recognize, that the people of the great valley are likely to be broader and more national in their views, less sectional, perhaps less provincial, than their brethren east and south.

It is a curious fact, that the leading minds of the late war—those who controlled events in civil and military affairs—most of them originated and were trained in the West. Lincoln, the master spirit, the representative American of the age, drawing his great ideas from the region of which he was the outgrowth; Chase, who, as a financier, was not inferior to the younger Pitt; Stanton, the war minister, of whom it has been so often said, as it was of Carnot, "He organized victory"; Grant, the ever-victorious; Sherman, whose pen was as sharp as his sword; the dashing Sheridan, the equal of the ablest of Napoleon's marshals—all of them, except Chase, born and raised west of the Alleghanies; and the Minister of Finance came so early to the West that its influence is clearly marked in his character.

What is done here, then, in this great central city of the continent, this half-way house between the two oceans, is to influence, for good or evil, our whole country, from sea to sea. The responsibility of a vast future is upon us. We cannot escape it. "No personal significance or insignificance," in the language of our great representative man, "can relieve us from it." What we do, or leave undone, will tell over a vast area and upon an untold future for good or evil. Let us rise to the magnitude of our position and our duties. Let us make this hall the receptacle of all the treasures of the past; let us gather here all that there is in the way of man's past history, which may serve to aid, guide, and to enlighten in the difficulties of the future. Within these walls the merchant, the artisan, the statesman may come, away from the noisy world outside, and commune with the great spirits of all ages. Here the poets, the moralists, the orators, the lawgivers, the philosophers, and statesmen of all ages and nations, may be consulted as guides and advisers. Here, especially, let us provide that every student of American history may follow our nation from its feeblest beginnings, through Indian, colonial, revolutionary, and progressive annals, down to and through the recent great drama of civil war; and doing this, we shall ourselves do something worthy of being remembered.

⟨ *The aspirations of Chicago come out in Isaac N. Arnold's remarks; its daily life, in 1868, is mirrored in local events reported in the same newspapers that described the Society's dedicatory meeting.*

DEATH OF W. L. NEWBERRY, ESQ.

The cable brings us the intelligence of the death of Walter L. Newberry, Esq., one of the oldest and most respected citizens of Chicago. The news is as surprising as it is painful, for Mr. Newberry, a few weeks ago, was in our midst in the enjoyment of his usual health. He left our city to enjoy the pleasures of an European trip, but died on the passage, expiring on the 6th inst. on board the steamer *Periere*, while she was en route from New York to Havre. A brief telegram, simply announcing the demise of the deceased, was received by his family yesterday.

EDWIN BOOTH AS OTHELLO

The fourth evening of Mr. Booth's engagement at McVicker's theater was characterized, last night, by the presentation of the great Shakespearean tragedy of "Othello," Booth playing the title role, and Miss McVicker taking the beautiful part of Desdemona. The audience was a very large and fashionable one, and the piece was put upon the stage in a most satisfactory manner.

MILITARY REUNION: AN APPEAL

To the Citizens of Chicago:

The Finance Committee of the Armies of the Tennessee, Cumberland, Ohio and Georgia are about to call upon you for pecuniary aid in defraying the expenses incident to the grand reunion of the officers of these armies, to be held in this city on the 15th and 16th of December.

The Committee is assured that there will be present Gens. Grant, Sherman, Sheridan, Thomas, Schofield, and with them a long and brilliant line of the most distinguished in the military history of our country. To the end that all things may be fitting, and that the reunion and entertainment of a body of gentlemen, among the noblest in the land, in our city, claiming soon to be the metropolis, may be alike creditable to you and us, we call upon you who, in darker hours, have never failed us, and who know that we are impecunious, to supply what we most need. We have never called in vain, and we believe we shall not now.

THE JAIL

There are at present one hundred and four prisoners in the jail, of whom twenty are females.

JANAUSHEK RECEPTION COMMITTEE

A meeting of the Janaushek reception committee was held last evening at Bauer's music store, Dr. Ernst Schmidt presiding. As Janaushek will not arrive in this city until the morning of the 30th of November, owing to her complying with the request of the citizens of Milwaukee to give an extra performance in their city, the ovation intended for the night of the 28th will be given on the night of the 30th inst., the occasion of her first performance in Chicago. It was resolved that the Germania Maennerchor be requested to sing on the occasion, which will take place in the Opera House. A finance committee consisting of Dr. Schmidt, E. Schlager, M. Radesky, Otto Peltzer, J. Bauer and Mr. Kresken, was appointed, and the meeting adjourned till Monday evening at 6 p.m.

(*The new building of the Chicago Historical Society soon took on the appearance of a treasure house. William Corkran describes the collections, not omitting, in accordance with his temperament, to point out the failings of his predecessor.*

. . . . The building was composed of three large rooms; the first or reading room a noble hall of ninety feet long by forty broad, and thirty-five feet in height, contained the collection of bound books. Of this collection, there were many volumes that were at once rare and costly. . . . .

In histories of States, the library was well supplied, having many rare works relating to the earliest histories of New York, Massachusetts, Virginia, and most of the Western States. Of the history of Chicago, the library contained volumes that . . . . can never be replaced. . . . .

Of the general collection of books, however . . . . , there is no doubt that the librarian had allowed his love of accumulating to overstep the limits of proper judgment. Thus it was that in this collection of 16,000 bound volumes . . . . at least half were of no manner of use, and simply an accumulation for which there was no demand. As an instance there were 2,000 volumes of old school books, which even as relics of bygone school days were of no value, owing to the large amount of duplicates they contained. Of the class of religion there were 7,320, of which 600 were old hymn books and prayer books, whilst 2,000 were books of sermons, which nobody had ever heard anything about, or were likely to be desirous of enquiring into. Next to these were some 1,500 Sunday school books, whilst again we had letters, memoirs, essays and other religious effusions from men whose minds were not calculated to produce the most enlightened changes in any dogma or ritual. That the Society should have encumbered itself with such material was a wonder to many who visited the rooms hoping to find the most simple works of reference which the library did not possess. . . . .

Although the collection of books in the reading room was not calculated to impress the casual visitor with very great interest, yet the appearance of the hall was indeed strikingly attractive. Hung around the walls was a noble collection of paintings, mostly the work of Mr. G. P. A. Healy, prominent among which was his masterpiece entitled, "Benjamin Franklin at the Court of Louis the Sixteenth." This picture was a grand work measuring some twenty feet square, representing that noblest of Americans standing in the simple attire of one of our representatives, holding in his hand his credentials, and seemingly urging upon the King the earnestness of our cause. The King, seated upon his throne, in the gaudy attire of monarchy, was a striking example of that effeminate court, around which were gathered numbers of gaily attired courtiers and ministers, who added by their silk and lace that stage-like appearance which we treat with such contempt. In the background was the Cardinal de Rohan, dressed in his long red robes, which so puzzled a young Chicago reporter that he described the picture as "Mr. and Mrs. Benjamin Franklin Being Introduced to General Washington."

The picture, however, was not only a masterpiece, but had attained a historic value in American art that can never be forgotten, having been the first picture, painted by an American artist, that had carried off the gold medal at the Exhibition held in Paris in 1856. After having been exhibited in some of the royal galleries in Europe, as also in the most prominent of the United States, and engravings taken, it was finally brought to Chicago by the artist, and there purchased by a society of gentlemen who formed themselves into the Art Gallery Association of Chicago. Through their efforts were gathered together a magnificent collection of valuable paintings, including most of Mr. Healy's principal works, as also a gem of Couture's, entitled "The Prodigal Son." The collection was finally deposited in the halls of the Historical Society, as their building was considered the only fireproof building in Chicago. It was here also that were grouped together Mr. Healy's original sketch of Daniel Webster replying to Hayne in the Senate in 1830, the large copy of which is now deposited in Faneuil Hall, Boston; also the original first paintings for the life-size portraits of Buchanan and Fillmore; that beautiful life-size portrait of Longfellow, so well known throughout the country owing to the many engravings that have been taken, as also those well known portraits of Miss Sneyd, the great English belle at the court of Napoleon, of La Fayette, Jefferson, Jackson, Daniel Webster, the Appletons, Colonel Thorne of New York, Colonel Washington, Burgess of Rhode Island, Davis of Massachusetts, and portraits of over three hundred celebrities whose names are well known to American history.

Hanging around the alcoves were the torn battle flags of those noble regiments that left Chicago, now treasured throughout the country by the thousands who had fought and bled under them, and who often would come to the hall, and as each soldier recognized his flag, his eye would brighten with emotion as he related some thrilling event in which he had taken part under this same emblem of war that now rested motionless and torn, a sacred memento of the past, which it was hoped would never again be touched by a rude hand, or exposed to any accident or injury. In their midst was grouped a collection of Rebel flags taken by these same regiments, and a desperate looking one was that of the Fort Benders, presented and woven for them by the ladies of that romantically named district. This flag was pierced through and through with bullet holes, whilst a large collection of Southern implements of warfare, composed of the most deadly looking knives, known as Southern toothpicks; swords made of scythes and bayonets of hoop iron, were arranged in order at the end of each flagstaff. Above was a no less valuable memento of the great rebellion than the bronze eagle that had stood over the flagstaff of Fort Sumter, which was said to have been knocked off by the first shot. This old relic, which had been saved by General Anderson and sent to Washington, had been subsequently presented to a Mr. Robb of St. Louis, who eventually presented it to the Historical Society of Chicago.

In another part of the Hall was one of Abraham Lincoln's favorite walking sticks, made from a rail that he is said to have split, and adorned with the horn of a buck shot by some old forester, who had had it handsomely mounted in silver and presented to Mr. Lincoln. In the room beneath was the original manuscript copy of the Emancipation Proclamation, written entirely by Mr. Lincoln and by him sent with an earnest and characteristic letter to the Sanitary Fair Commission, to be sold by them for the benefit of the soldiers. There it was first raffled off by so many shares, amounting altogether to ten thousand dollars, and subsequently purchased of the winner by a Mr. Bryan, president of the Soldiers' Home, who sent it to the Historical Society, as it was thought that there at least, it would be safe. . . . .

More satirically, Corkran describes what went on in the Society's building. The two old pioneers who aroused his superior laughter were undoubtedly Gurdon S. Hubbard and John H. Kinzie.

. . . . A meeting of the Historical Society was generally a very staid, stiff, and uninteresting affair. The proceedings generally consisted in the President's calling the meeting to order, when the Librarian or Secretary would read his reports, also the correspondence received during the month, concluding by offering some suggestions for the benefit of the institution. These suggestions were generally referred to a committee composed of three gentlemen who beyond having their names recorded in the books and newspapers never gave the subject a thought.

So soon as this part of the performance was gone through, a general discussion was entered into, either upon religious subjects, transactions in real estate, or little interchanges of mutual admiration, especially passed upon the wealthier members. It was indeed amusing sometimes, when the meetings were largely attended, to notice the total absence of all interest shown for literary matters, or for the benefit of the institution, and the large amount of self-approbation that reigned amongst all.

Once, however, we succeeded in awakening a spark of interest, by reading a letter from a gentleman asking some information regarding the Pottawotomie Indians.

One member recollected having seen these noble representatives of a long-ago-killed-off race straggling along the borders of Lake Michigan in full war paint and feathers. They were a noble and warlike people living entirely upon the produce of the chase, which they generally brought to old Fort Dearborn at the beginning of winter, where a general barter took place between them and the authorized agents.

It was then that a prim old settler, who rarely opened his mouth, gave a broad grin and a humph, upon which the president asked him to relate his experiences.

He had known the Pottawotomies, who were always at war with the Wyandotes and Peories, who in turn when defeated were always attacked by the Sacs and Foxes, so-called

*❨ The Marine Bank Building,
corner of Lake and La Salle
streets. Here, in the office
of J. Y. Scammon, the Society
was organized in 1856.*

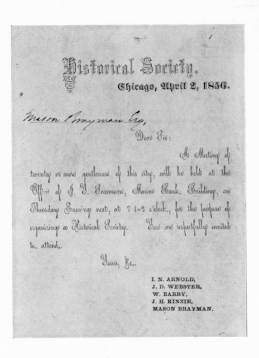

*❨ Invitation to "twenty or
more gentlemen of this city,"
to form a Historical Society.*

(*William Corkran's Chicago: A view of the State Street bridge as it appeared in 1868, before the Great Fire.*

(*William Corkran's Chicago: The north side of Randolph Street, east from Clark Street, in 1868.*

❲ *The Reverend William Barry, Jr., founder, first Secretary and first Librarian of the Chicago Historical Society. Below, William H. Brown, the first President.*

Albert Edward.
Prince of Wales.

❡ *The home of William H. Brown, 120 South Michigan Avenue, where the Society often met in its early years.*
At left, the Prince of Wales as he appeared when he visited the Society in 1860.

*⟨ Isaac N. Arnold, President of the
Society, 1876–1884, and the architect's drawing
of the Society's building that
was opened in 1868
and destroyed in 1871.*

Typical scenes in 1868: The east side of Clark Street looking south from Madison. Police escorting "femmes de joie" to the magistrate's court in the Armory and Gas Works.

《 *Mrs. J. Y. Scammon, one of the first two women to be elected members of the Society.*

《 *Leonard W. Volk and his busts of Lincoln and Douglas. Below, Volk's plaster model of Lincoln's head now owned by the Society.*

from their bagging all property on which they could lay
their hands, and Foxes from their cunning. Often and often
did the agents learn that a party of Pottawotomies were returning laden with the spoils of the chase, and that their trail
had been traced to Fort Dearborn. The agents then would
enter into a compact with the Sacs and Foxes to follow them,
and whilst they proceeded in the direction of the Pottawotomie village, carrying demijohns and bottles of forty-rod
whiskey, also pipes and tobacco, and very rarely money, they
would desire the Foxes to wait until the whole encampment
were intoxicated and then to fall upon them, and take away
their skins and also their scalps. . . . .

A most amusing incident took place at this meeting, which
from the solemn manner in which it was performed, almost
choked the poor librarian to death from suppressed laughter.

A discussion had arisen between two of the old ex-
traders regarding the modes and habits of the Pottawotomies.
One insisted that after every feast, a general sacred dance
would take place, in which sometimes one or two thousand
men would participate, and from the regular and peculiar
tramp, tramp, accompanied by the loud murmuring grunt or
wail with which they begin their religious exercises, would
give vent to their feelings in such a manner that the sound
could be heard miles away, whilst the hunter, by putting his
ear to the ground, could sometimes tell the ceremony they
were performing miles off, by the peculiar tread.

Upon this, a discussion arose as to the manner in which
the Indians turned out their feet, one old settler affirming
that on the contrary they always turned them in. The first
settler, now fairly mad at his authority being questioned,
awoke from his customary lethargy and sprang forward to

show how it was done.

Imagine an old, grey haired veteran, doubled up as if he had a colic, his hands akimbo, his legs stretched out as wide as they could go, his head half raised as he performed the Indian dance, which consisted of a slow motion of the body, accompanied by a low grunting sound resembling the "humph, humph" of a dying elephant.

The excitement now of the meeting was intense, for the other old pioneer of the West sprang forward with that innate jealousy burning in his heart which is warmed by the Indian recollections, and seemingly crouching forward, as if he were about to tomahawk the first, he also joined in the dance, adopting quite an opposite attitude and motion. The two men kept moving round and round the room, presenting the most ludicrous appearance, when a third came forward and showed how the early Sacs performed the sacred *can can*.

The performance, done in so solemn a manner, was almost killing, for the motions of three venerable descendants of the Prairies resembled the sudden attack of cholera on three very modest persons. The other members sat staring silently, and some admiringly, upon the scene, which continued till at last the exhibitors, panting and breathless, sat down silently, awaiting the opinion of the others.

The president thanked them for their able illustrations, and remembered well having seen a like exhibition, but not having made the Indian a particular study, he could not tell which was right. . . . . The meeting was brought suddenly to a close, as we felt it necessary to retire where we could enjoy a quiet laugh. . . . .

❨ *The Society breaks with tradition. Minutes of meetings held on February 15 and March 16, 1870, record the revolutionary step.*

. . . . The names of several ladies were proposed for membership. As they will undoubtedly be elected they will constitute the initiatory lady members of the Society. . . . .

. . . . The names of Mrs. Maria S. Scammon and Miss Jessie L. Bross having been proposed at the last meeting for membership, an election was ordered, Gov. Bross acting as teller. They were unanimously elected. They were also enrolled as life members, together with Louis Sapieha, Marcus A. Farwell, and Robert E. Moss. The list of life members now contains 55 names, the initiation fees constituting a life membership fund of $15,500.

❨ *The Society acquires a valuable addition to its collection, and with the acquisition, an interesting contribution to Lincoln biography.*

. . . . Hon. I. N. Arnold read an interesting letter from Leonard W. Volk, the sculptor, dated Rome, Feb. 22nd, [1870], and requesting the reception by the Society of his familiar and faithful bust of Lincoln. Mr. Volk says he is rejoiced to know that the bust had been secured by the Society, and more particularly so because it is in the same city where the immortal subject gave the sittings for the model in clay, and where Mr. Volk chiselled it from a block of Carrara marble which he imported expressly from Italy, it being the first of the kind sent directly to Chicago.

The sittings for the bust, about twelve altogether, were

given by Mr. Lincoln in April, 1860, at the time he was employed as counsel with Mr. Arnold in the United States District Court in this city. He had promised these sittings two years before, when Mr. Volk first met him during the canvass between him and Mr. Douglas at Lincoln, Ill., when they were on their way to Springfield, at which place the latter made one of his opening speeches of the memorable campaign of 1858.

The sittings were held in Mr. Volk's studio in the Portland Block, and he says that "of all the sittings I ever received those of Mr. Lincoln were the most interesting as I felt a presentiment at the time that he whose features I was endeavoring to portray in the clay would soon be President of the U. S., and under circumstances so exciting in the history of our country. Therefore I was desirous of making a faithful representation of him without a wish to flatter his remarkably rugged and striking features, but make *him just as he was*, so that posterity might look at it, and know it as a veritable and faithful likeness.

"I took a cast of his face in plaster at the time which greatly aided me when he was not present, this cast and his two hands . . . . I now have in my studio . . . . , and I intend making use of them in the execution of a colossal statue of Mr. Lincoln."

The following contributed to the fund for the purchase of the bust: I. N. Arnold, E. H. Sheldon, Mark Skinner, B. W. Raymond, J. H. Dunham, Wm. Blair, J. Y. Scammon, Geo. Schneider, John C. Haines, L. Z. Leiter, L. Tilton, C. P. Kellogg, E. S. Isham, A. H. Burley, John H. Tyrrell, and the Chicago Tribune Co.

DISASTER

1871 – 1874

❲ *ON Saturday, October 7, 1871, fire breaks out in a planing mill at Canal and Jackson streets, and for a time threatens the dry, ramshackle city with a major disaster. By heroic efforts the firemen bring the blaze under control, but not until it has destroyed four square blocks of buildings.*

Twenty-four hours later Mrs. Patrick O'Leary's cow barn, 137 De Koven Street, goes up in flames. This time there is no reprieve.

One month after the Great Fire, William Corkran, in self-exculpation, describes his efforts to save the Chicago Historical Society.

CARE OF THE ASTOR LIBRARY
LA FAYETTE PLACE
NEW YORK CITY, N. Y.,
Novbr. 7th, '71

E. H. Sheldon Esq.
President
Chicago Historical Society
DEAR SIR:

Great was my astonishment today, to learn from a friend just arrived from Chicago, that Mr. Arnold and other members of the late Historical Society had censured me for not making a report regarding the terrible and sudden destruction of that building, which I believe you all know I was devotedly attached to. . . . .

I will now submit the following synopsis of a full report I drew up on my arrival in New York, as I intend to publish my notes, in vindication of the slurs cast upon me, without my first having been called upon to explain, or even having been asked to do so, although prior to leaving Chicago I addressed you a note stating the causes that compelled my leaving your city without first seeing you—and as I understand that Doctor Barry was immediately nominated and appointed your secretary and librarian, I will ask you to do me the kindness and justice to read the following carefully, and to judge for yourself, whether I have not had your interests at heart throughout.

On Saturday October the 6th [7th] I called upon Mr. William Hickling at his residence on Calumet Avenue, in relation to the Manuscript of Mr. Flowers, as also some letters he had requested me a few days previous to allow him to look over. As I was returning home, I witnessed the fearful conflagration of that night, and assisted in throwing lumber into the river, until about 3 a.m. On Sunday night as I returned from Divine Service, I heard the alarm bells, but being too tired out from my previous night's labors, determined to rest, so as to be up betimes on the next morning for work. At eleven o'clock the alarms continuing I got up and proceeded down town and was standing by the gas works, when it was blown up and my coat torn off my back. Picking up a coat found in the streets I pushed back with the crowd and met Mr. Scammon and General Strong opposite the Court House. The fire had now assumed such awful dimensions, that I concluded to return to the North Side. In endeavoring to pass through La Salle Street Tunnell, I was almost smothered up by the smoke and crowd, and forcing my way back, found that Dearborn Street was already ablaze, and the fire fiercely driving up the North Side. When I reached State Street Bridge, it was on fire, and I believe I was the last person who dared go through it. I then dashed on to the Historical Society and found that already persons had opened the cellar door, and were stowing away property and valuables. Firmly believing that the old building would stand, I encouraged our neighbors, who now were assembled round us, to place for safe keeping whatever valuable material they wished to save. These persons were Mr. Gerard, Mr. Griffin, Doctor Freer, who placed a box of valuable instruments, Mr. Abel, General Webster, and Major Kinzie. I felt it scarcely human to refuse at so awful a time the shelter for the remains of the few valuables these people could save, and I believe the Society would have sanctioned my endeavors. My old janitor having now arrived, he and I proceeded at once to secure all the buckets of water we could, in case the sidewalk took fire. I offered him and two men, fifty dollars apiece, to go on the roof, and soak it with water; both tried but could not, owing to the sparks and embers that fell upon the poor fellows' hands. Colonel Stone now arriving refused to allow anybody to enter the cellar, as many now kept piling in trunks and furniture. At this time the sidewalk began to smoke, the wind was awful, Mr. Griffin's house and the whole row opposite were on fire, and the heat excessive. Still I remained at my post, and now I and John began pouring water on the sidewalk, some men who had assisted us fled, as they were frightened, and yelled to me to leave off, as they said the building was doomed. Not believing this,

I told John to remain with me, and I would pay him. Colonel Stone however had his back to the door and refused to allow John in, to get water. I was already tired out and begged Colonel not to oppose me. Receiving no encouragement I now seized a shovel and wheel barrow, and John and I, in that awful heat, still managed to throw four wheel barrows full of earth upon the sidewalk. Had I had more assistance I believe this means would have saved the cellar. It was however too late, as the flames now had caught the stairs and there was no hope remaining.

As a last effort, I now made up my mind to save what I could in the building, and for that purpose burst open the door. John and I now removed Abraham Lincoln's bust from its stand on the table, and placed it in a corner, where when the ruins are examined I think it will be found in either the catch basin or sewer, or else immured under the middle window. At this time a number of half-frightened women rushed in, and implored shelter. I told them I did not know if the building would stand, but so long as it did, they might remain, as I would myself. John and I then removed the Emancipation Proclamation, which I carried upstairs, and wrapped up, in the old battle flags, which I tore off their poles, so as to save them. I also took Abraham Lincoln's walking stick, and some of Mr. Healy's smaller pictures down, thinking if the worst came to the worst, that at least we could save something.

Whilst I was engaged with John, the women suddenly rushed upstairs, shrieking that the rooms beneath were all on fire. At the same time there were two violent explosions which shook the building and hardly a moment seemed to have elapsed before the skylight windows came crashing in, and the roof [was] all in one blaze of fire. John and I were then standing near the staircase, and both of us fairly jumped downstairs at one bound. Dashing through the lecture room, now one blaze of fire, communicated from the back onto the stage, we both forced ourselves through a window, and jumped onto Mr. Gerard's garden. Here everything was awful—the houses all round us, before us, and behind were on fire, and the heat terrible. John's body, I believe was found in the ruins a few days after, showing how narrow an escape I had. What became of the women who were in the building, God alone knows.

I then rushed back to my boarding house and got an old man to assist me in getting out my trunk, as this house was already on fire. So that I lost my own library, and a good many valuable letters and papers.

I dragged my trunk to Mr. Burling's house, who with noble kindness, which I shall never forget, gave me shelter, and something to eat.

Ask Mr. Burling, if I looked as if I had been idle. Ask him if I did not tell him immediately the story I am now writing to you—and I believe Mr. Burling will certify to every word I now write. I did not believe Colonel Stone could have escaped, as the stairs must have come crashing down, half an hour after I last saw him, whilst the hen house at the back, was on fire when I first entered the building.

In conculsion, Sir, let me state that after leaving Mr. Burling's house I met Mr. Scudder, who told me Mr. Arnold's house was gone—from that point I steered south on Wells Street, and again forced my way to Clark at the corner of Ontario, and saw that the Historical Society was down, as also the Clarendon House. This was about eight a.m.—so I should judge. . . . .

From Monday to Wednesday, I was downtown hunting up Mr. Scammon, and heard on that day, that you were expected in Friday, from New York. I had now lost everything, with the exception of my overcoat. My coat, trowsers, vest, were burned off my back, and I had to borrow all round for a change. Mr. Boss [Bross?] was the first man who gave me a meat meal from Sunday night, whilst a Mr. Brennan gave me a dollar. I did not lose my pluck, but having nowhere to go to, or no place to sleep in, I thought I should leave Chicago for a time, until you were prepared to receive me again. I called upon you on Saturday, you were out, it was pouring rain, and I was drenched through. Mr. Beckwith told me he could not give me shelter any more, whilst the members of the Society I met, such as Mr. Dunham, had not the humanity to offer me a crust of bread. Mr. Scammon saw me on Saturday, after I had been three days looking out for him. He was as usual kind in his manner, and would I feel have assisted me if he could. He asked me to fill two water carts for him, which I did, as his men will attest. When I again went to look for him, no one knew where I could find him. . . . .

In conclusion let me state, that when I arrived here, I distinctly told my friends I was going to return as soon as I had had a refit of clothes. This was soon given me, as also one thousand dollars. But my friends now urged me not to return but to stay here at least through the winter. I was introduced to Mr. J. Carson Brevoort, who at once asked me to enter the Astor Library. . . . .

I am now, Sir, in a position that will make me a more

thorough and practical librarian, and I feel sure, Sir, that there are few persons who would wish me ill of my success. I did not boast to Mr. Brevoort of what I could do, but I told him of our losses. Mr. Brevoort immediately informed me, that I could write to you to draw up a letter, asking the assistance of New York men to rebuild the Society, that he would himself head the list, give books, and thought $45,000 could be thus raised. I have since seen other persons of influence and wealth to whom I have been introduced, and I had hoped shortly to have been able to write to you a happy account of my doings.

In my attempts at saving your property I lost everything I owned in the world. Not a member of the institution offered me any assistance, my salary which was due I have not claimed. I delayed giving you particulars of what I had done and now, Sir, I learn that I have been censured by the Society, not one of which came near to see what I was about.

In the name of justice and humanity, I ask that my conduct during the fire be carefully examined. I ask that poor John's remains be claimed as a witness, and now Sir, I ask you finally to give me a letter certifying that I have ever faithfully, honorably, manfully done my best in your interests, and remain

Yours very obediently,

W. CORKRAN.*

---

* *Corkran continued to play in hard luck, or, if one prefers, to reap the reward of a difficult personality. On May 17, 1955, Mr. Rutherford D. Rogers, Chief of the Reference Department, New York Public Library, responded as follows to an appeal for information:*

"On March 4, 1873, the Sun *carried an article, 'Astor Library Troubles, the Mutilation of the Costliest Works, Demoralization in the Building.' It*

It is obvious that during the fire, if not before, there was friction in plenty between Corkran and Samuel Stone, the Assistant Librarian. Stone tells his side of the story in a letter to William Barry, serving again as the Society's Secretary.

CHICAGO, March 26, 1872

Revd. Wm. Barry,
Secretary of the Chicago Historical Society.
DEAR SIR,

Allow me to state some facts of the burning of the Chicago Historical Society building Oct. 9, 1871. As life is uncertain and believing I was the last person [who] left it, I have penned all facts from entering [to] leaving the building that came to my knowledge. I do not wish to come into controversy with others who have made statements, nor to have my letter appear sensational to call sympathy, but to be credited, if thought worthy, after reading the accompanying statement.

Herewith is my brief facts & escape from Chicago Historical Society building and my doings while there.

Between 1 and 2 o'clock on the morning of the 9th of Oct. 1871 I was awakened by severe ringing of my house

---

included the following statement: 'The facilities offered for these vandalisms are largely increased by the distrust of Mr. Straznicky, the librarian, toward his subordinates. One of the assistant librarians complains that when a mutilation or loss is discovered and reported to Mr. Straznicky, the gentleman at once charges the offence upon the person who informs him of it, and hence very few cases of depredation are reported at all.' William Corkran, an assistant librarian, admitted to the Board that he had given this information to the Sun reporter, whereupon the Board instructed the secretary to inform Mr. Corkran that his services would not be needed after April 30. . . . .
"Corkran drops out of New York directories after 1872–73 and no record of his death ever appeared in the New York Evening Post. He apparently left New York for parts unknown."

bell. On jumping out of bed, I was told "the city was on fire." About 2 o'clock I made from my house No. 612 North Clark Street,* south about one & half miles—there found Clark Street bridge on fire and all eastward towards the lake enveloped in flame.

I then returned north to the Historical Society rooms. Mr. Wm. Corkran, the librarian in charge, was receiving trunks, boxes and bundles through the basement cellar door. About 3 o'clock sparks of fire were flying near the building. I thought it prudent to prevent any more goods liable to ignite to be deposited—particularly cotton bundles. I told Mr. Corkran the danger. I then immediately took charge of the basement door. Mr. Corkran left for outside, packages continued to come, pressing urgently to be admitted. Duty and danger warranted me stubbornly [to] refuse to open the door. Consequently much abuse toward me. As I could not close the door to lock it (some object at the bottom outside prevented) I was obliged to press against it. After a few minutes Mr. Corkran sang out to me from outside to allow the janitor to the hydrant (in basement cellar) for two pails of water, saying "the sidewalk [is] on fire." He was admitted but I have no further recollection about him.

Few minutes after a Mrs. Stone in the family of Mr. E. W. Griffin opposite of the Society building, was the last person [to] come to the door with a loud voice through the roaring wind calling me by name and giving her name begging me to receive a small box. I received it saying something that I was in danger—few minutes previous two voices calling me to come out—I was in danger. Believing the

---

* *Between Schiller Street and North Avenue.*

building was in danger and as soon as I could leave, I canted a trunk against the door & made for the north end of the basement cellar. I mounted the upper shelf of newspapers, lying on my back with my feet closed the northwest basement (4 light) windows. Here I observed in the rear, every part of the yard and the heavens full of flying sparks and some fire brands. I next hurried up one flight of stairs into the reception room, thence up another flight into the upper library room.

At this moment a terrible blast of wind, fire and smoke filled the entire Ontario Street in front. The entire casement of the front window was in a blaze, hanging like feathers on every inch of the window. I immediately hurried down into the reception room to get the record book and Lincoln Proclamation. Not finding the record book I attempted to break the frame containing the Proclamation to take from it the Proclamation and fold it under my coat, it being in a stout frame. Not a moment more to stop. Abandoned the frame. At this moment again the wind and fire filled the whole heavens frightfully, dashing fire brands against the reception room windows. A chinking I heard seemed from above, probably from the upper window or roofing broke in. Believing a minute more to try to save the Proclamation would be too late for my escape, I next made for the basement door, stamped fire out of two bundles and canted back the trunk to escape. The strong suffocation from smoking bundles outside of basement door prevented. I then tore open the third bundle (smoking), snatched from it a shawl, covered my head and sprang out with [as] much speed as possible, leaving the door little open. I could not shut it.

At a glance I could see the steps overhead, the sidewalk,

front fence, Mr. Girard cottage and every building south
in one mass of blaze & firebrands flying furiously. My only
escape was to the rear of Mr. Girard cottage in a midst of
dense smoke. Not a moment to feel for the gate. With a
bound upon a box or something next to the fence I sprang
over the low picket fence into Dearborn Street. At this
moment a blaze, probably from Mr. Girard building, struck
me with force. I felt it to my skin. I dropt my burnt
shawl and ran to the corner of Erie St., following me in
the middle Dearborn St. a bellowing cow with scorched
back. Again another terrible blast of wind forced the poor
cow out of sight in dark smoke to the east. I purposely
dropt down on my hands [to] prevent being blown down for
such was the force. I next made to mount one of the high
stone steps of the three brick buildings facing south on Erie
Street between Dearborn and North Clark Street directly
in rear of Chicago Historical Society building, to take the
last look of the destruction of our fifteen (15) years of
labor of valuable gatherings. The entire front, top & sides
of the building was in one mass of flame and everything
surrounding. It was painful to see it. The heat being too
intense, I was obliged to leave to the west. There were no
persons near me. All the houses were abandoned.

As I came to the corner of Dearborn and Erie Street
from the Society building, a woman was running directly
east into the fire. I understood a woman was found burnt
near there. At this moment a great blast of wind and smoke,
seemingly a blaze of about 200 to 300 feet in length, perhaps 150 feet in height, passed nearly over me little to the
right making N. E. diagonally, pouring the entire volume
over two entire blocks into the top of the spire of the Church

of Holy Name, situated east side of State Street between Huron and Superior Sts. In an instant the top was in a blaze. There were moments I could see buildings appear to melt down from three to five minutes. Such sights I never saw before.

Had I known the speed and heat of the coming fire, I could have left my post at the basement door earlier and secured the records and Proclamation. The unprecedented calamity was beyond all of my experience. Another fact worth noticing. While I was on the high stone steps on Erie St., I saw the entire west side of the Society building in one great sheet of blaze burning apparently every brick. There was no woodwork on that side of the building. The fact of Mrs. Stone above mentioned calling me by name and giving her name in the hearing of persons near her gave reason of some to [tell] the Press that "Old Col. Stone and wife perished." In regard to others sheltered in the Chi. Hist. Soc. fireproof building supposed perished. If there, they would have been seen by me, unless they were hidden in the Lecture room and in the wash room. It is fair to presume I was the last person [who] left the Chicago Historical building.

Mr. E. W. Griffin, owner of the buildings south side and opposite the Society building on Ontario St. remaining, so he told me, to the last in and near his houses, backing north by the force of heat on Dearborn St. and knowing I was in the Society building and but one way to escape— not seeing me, presumed I had perished.

Very truly yours,

SAM. STONE

(The status of the Society for three years after the fire is succinctly indicated by one brief letter in its files.

CHICAGO & NORTH WESTERN RAILWAY CO.
LOCAL TREASURER'S OFFICE

CHICAGO Feby 17 1874

E. H. Sheldon, Esq
DEAR SIR—

Will you have the kindness to inform me if there is a "Historical Society" in the City and how I would address a communication to reach the same.

Yours truly

A. B. HULL

C & NW Ry Gen Office

Room 19

The remains from the Fire and what has been gathered since, are in charge of Doct. Boyesen, in Scammon Court, in rear of 16 Congress Street. *[Unsigned]*

A few days later President Sheldon receives a communication that must have given him heart. Through the will of Mrs. Gilpin, Henry D. Gilpin's benevolent intentions would be carried out, at least in part. The Chicago Historical Society, moribund, might be restored to health.

THE HISTORICAL SOCIETY OF PENNSYLVANIA
NO. 820 SPRUCE STREET

PHILADELPHIA, Febry 19th 1874

DEAR SIR:

It is with regret that I communicate to you the fact of the death of Mrs. Gilpin, widow of the late Henry D. Gilpin.

She died on the 12th of this month and was buried on Monday last in the same grave with her husband.

Mrs. Gilpin's will provides that in case the will of Mr. Gilpin is successfully contested, that the sum of $40,000 shall go to the three Societies. Her will is very long & I have read it only very hurriedly.

I write to let you know that Mr. Charles Gilpin, executor of H. D. G., has filed his account, which has been referred to Mr. George Junkin, Auditor, who will be ready in five or six weeks to act. At that time it will be necessary for you to appear before him by counsel and make claim on behalf of the Chicago Historical Society. Mr. Theodore Cuyler will represent the Academy of the Fine Arts and desires me to say to you that if you desire it he will do what he can for you.

Our Council has not yet met, and therefore I cannot speak on our part.

Very truly yours

TOWNSEND WARD

Secretary

Mrs. Gilpin had not only made provision for the Chicago Historical Society and the two Pennsylvania institutions if her husband's will should be successfully contested; she had also done everything she could to make sure that it would not be contested. In her own will she had made generous bequests to members of the Gilpin family, but in each instance had stipulated that the bequest would be void if any attempt were made to thwart her husband's wishes by contesting his will.

The situation pointed to a long and expensive lawsuit

of uncertain outcome. Good sense dictated compromise. Running counter to the legendary behavior of Philadelphia lawyers, George W. Biddle, representing the Gilpins, decided to bring about a fair and amicable settlement.

The Secretary of the Historical Society of Pennsylvania keeps President Sheldon informed.

THE HISTORICAL SOCIETY OF PENNSYLVANIA
NO. 820 SPRUCE STREET

PHILADELPHIA, April 21, 1874

DEAR SIR:

I had a conversation this evening with Mr. George W. Biddle who represents four of the Gilpins; all except William. He first of all expressed his very great gratification that his kinsman Craig Biddle had appeared, and advised that I should say to him that he would like a free conversation with a view to a speedy settlement, and that no one was better calculated than Craig to effect it. After this, which so entirely coincides with my own judgment, resulting from an intimacy of many years, I feel no hesitation in urging you to have Craig Biddle to represent you permanently. . . . .

George W. Biddle said to me that he had had the affair in his hands for some years, and had thoroughly studied the case. He agreed with us as to the question about the unsold property in Chicago, not as a matter of course following in its descent the law of domicile, and I agreed with him that if Henry D. Gilpin were living he would make larger provision for his family, in view of his estate proving larger than he anticipated, and the value of money less than it was in his day. He asked me what was the value of the residuary estate of H. D. G. I told him $330,000, indeed more, as the unsold lots were appraised only at their assessed value. He then said the three Societies were in the same boat, and if a division were made $170,000 for the Societies would certainly be a very handsome thing. It is apparent therefore that Mr. Biddle contemplates what you spoke of, an equal division; and he further told me that he had already sent a power of attorney to Syria for Miss Gilpin (Mary I believe) to sign. With regard to William Gilpin's interest, he said if there were any trouble with him, an arrangement could be effected as to the four-fifths.

All this is so gratifying, although what I expected from such a man as George Biddle, that I cannot help at once communicating it to you. I have done so freely, and only ask you to hold it so far confidential as not to too freely publish it. I mean communicate it only to such as are interested, and let it be clearly understood that he spoke to me as a friend, and not as counsel on behalf of his client. Geo. Biddle, however, is not the man to say a word that he would not stand by.

I am very truly yours
TOWNSEND WARD

A month later Craig Biddle, the Society's counsel in Philadelphia, was ready with a compromise to which all parties would eventually subscribe.

PHILADA May 20 1874

Edwin H. Sheldon
Prest Historical Society of Chicago
MY DEAR SIR

I enclose you a draft of a compromise of the claims under

the will of Henry D. Gilpin, Esq., upon which I desire yr instructions.

In a litigation, I think our bequests here wd be declared void. As far as regards the Real Estate in Chicago, in regard to which all three societies are on the same footing, if it was awarded to us, it would be subject to the trusts of the will. It is therefore proposed (the legacy to Mrs. Gilpin being deducted) to divide the residue between the heirs and the three societies or to give the heirs $200,000, the Societies to take the rest. In order to do this the auditor before whom the case is now pending, would have to decide in favor of the heirs and they would then convey our share to us free of all restrictions whatsoever. So that valuing the whole estate at $500,000 there would be, less the amount bequeathed to Mrs. Gilpin, say $400,000 to divide or $200,000 between the three societies.

I think our societies will agree here, preferring very much the smaller amount, free of all restrictions, to a lawsuit to obtain a larger amount subject to troublesome conditions.

To carry out this plan we must of course have an adverse decision by the auditor as the Trustees could not compromise our claim.

We would of course have a claim under Mrs. Gilpin's will should the auditor decide in favor of the heirs. The disposition of the Societies here, however, is to consider our receiving a large amount from the estate of Mr. Gilpin, a reason morally, for not claiming what Mrs. Gilpin wd probably in that event have left to her own family and they would be disposed to ask from the $100,000 only from fifteen to twenty to be divided between the three societies.

It is very necessary to act promptly in this matter while

the matter can be controlled & before any new complications arise. . . . .

Very respectfully
CRAIG BIDDLE

❮[For hours, on the afternoon and evening of July 14, 1874, Chicago appeared to be doomed a second time by fire. This time the blaze broke out, about 4:15, at Taylor and Clark streets. Before its spread was stopped, the fire devastated an irregular area between Van Buren and Twelfth streets on the north and south, and between Michigan Avenue and Clark Street east and west. It destroyed 800 buildings, mostly frame, caused losses of $3,000,000, and generated panics all too familiar to those who remembered 1871.

The Tribune *fills its issue of July 15 with a remarkably detailed and vivid account.*

[Time: mid-evening.]

. . . . From the top of the residence of Thomas Hoyne, No. 267 Michigan avenue, a sight was seen over the flames which extended from Polk street to the Post-Office, which was grand and awful beyond description. The whole burnt area was still alive with fire, while the main torrent was sweeping with terrific force northward. The volume of sparks circled and fell far out in the lake, and as far north as eye could reach through the dense smoke. The spire of the First Baptist Church stood high above the general volume of fire, and from it a thin stream of flames like a fiery banner shot outward. . . . .

The Post-Office seemed to prove hardly any impediment to the flames. It burnt in an incredible space of time, and gave forth a heat that soon set fire to buildings farther north.

The great throng of people who had been burned out, or were in danger, were crowding towards the lake shore, carrying, pulling, pushing, and wheeling in every conceivable manner their loads of household goods. The down-town vehicles were pushing southward, while in the minds of the apprehensive the part north of the fire seemed doomed to immediate destruction. . . . .

The wind came swooping down towards the circle of flames in such power as to almost carry people off their feet. A blackness gathered over the lake, and the lurid torrents of fire streamed upward from the burning buildings in a manner both majestic and terrifying. Everyone seemed to give up hope, and conceded that, with such a volume of air back of it, the flames must be driven into the heart of the city, and that the scene of general destruction would be repeated. . . . .

All along the boundary of the fire the crowds were enormous, and the lake shore appeared a solid mass of human beings. From an early hour in the evening, North Clark, Dearborn, and Wells were crowded with vehicles filled with furniture and other goods which were being conveyed to the remotest portion of the city for safety.

About 6 o'clock Michigan avenue, from Congress to Twelfth street, became gorged with teams, presenting a sight not unlike that witnessed on the morning of Oct. 9, 1871. Loads of household furniture on drays, truck-wagons, express-wagons, and handcarts, light buggies and hacks loaded with trunks, foot passengers with great bundles on their shoulders, filled the whole street, all moving southward, while the cross streets were pouring a continuous stream into the mass. The gorge would move a dozen steps and then come to a halt, and then start again and close up against an obstruction; but good nature prevailed all along the whole line, and in the end all the teams got out of the range of the fire.

Lake Park was early pre-empted by poor people who could get no teams or who had not the means of transportation, and this convenient and ample space presented a sorry sight of trunks, bundles, household utensils, and clothing, with their dejected proprietors ruefully watching the little they had saved. . . . .

The scene on Fourth avenue, in the vicinity of Harrison and Polk streets, about 9 o'clock, was one that entirely baffles any attempt at accurate description. The people were as panic-stricken as when, on the 9th of October three years ago, they fled for their lives before the fire-fiend. The sidewalks were rendered impassable by the crowds which congregated from every quarter, and the streets were blocked by the furniture which was transferred from every house in the vicinity.

Expressmen and hackmen reaped a rich harvest, and as usual took every opportunity to "bleed" the unfortunate persons who, many of them for the second time within the past three years, were rendered homeless and destitute. As high as twenty and twenty-five dollars was asked to transfer a single load of furniture for a few blocks, and in more than one instance the exorbitant charge was willingly paid. There were others, however, composed of that class of individuals who have made this part of Chicago a bye-word and a reproach for years past, who took the calamity as a mere matter of course—a little worse, perhaps, than a "pull," but still a matter to be dealt with in a philosophical manner—"a thing that can't be helped, you know; let it rip," as a colored female of doubtful virtue observed to a bystander. Scores of houses of this character were abandoned by their inmates without any attempt to remove either their furniture or personal property, and in more than one case coarse jokes were indulged in as the flames angrily seized their prey.

The saloons all round the vicinity of the new burnt district reaped a huge harvest. They were thronged all evening with a thirsty and blasphemous crowd, who vied with each other in abusing the Fire Department, discussing the causes of the fire, and in "hoisting" into their stomachs the fiery compounds for which the saloons of the district are so famous.

Inflamed by liquor, with no fear of Rehm's men in blue before their eyes, the roughs had full sway, and fights and altercations abounded. At every corner some peaceable citizen received the "bounce," and in several cases general fights followed. The majority of these, however, were promptly suppressed by the bystanders, who formed themselves into amateur vigilance committees and did their utmost to protect both life and property. . . . .

The culmination and end of the fire was in the middle of the solid brick block on the west side of Wabash avenue, between Van Buren and Adams streets. Here, on each side of the broad avenue, was a solid brick-front five stories in height. If the fire should cross Wabash avenue it would inevitably destroy at least a million dollars' worth of property, including the Gardner House, the Matteson Hotel, the Exposition Building, and a massive row of business fronts.

The Fire Department evidently saw that this was a vital point, and the crisis of the catastrophe; and it was nothing else than grand to see the concentrated power of forty engines brought to bear upon this small space. The flames would ever and anon leap up and span the street as if determined to devour the structures in their front. The next instant they would sink in a mass of steam and smoke, to burst out again after a moment's repression, with fully renewed vigor. The broad avenue was packed solid with people, all of whom fully grasped the importance of the crisis. Probably 100,000 people witnessed the grand culmination and close of this battle between fire and water. . . . .

The last important buildings to fall before the flames were those owned by J. Young Scammon at the southeastern corner of the devastated area. The Tribune *writer was doubtless unaware that what remained of the Chicago Historical Society's possessions was lost in the destruction of the Scammon properties.*

On Wabash avenue, next but one to the corner of Congress street, Mr. J. Y. Scammon had erected a handsome brick building, five stories high, which was known as the Inter-Oceanic Building. In the rear of this was the Marine Bank Building, and on Michigan avenue his own charming residence. This block of buildings formed a small city in itself. Business and residence were gathered almost beneath the same roof. The destruction of these buildings was a terrible blow to Mr. Scammon—a culmination, it is sincerely to be hoped, of the bad luck which has recently dogged him. He lost an immense sum of money here in the great fire, and the fates might have taken this into consideration. But they did not. The greatest loss he feels was that of his library. He saved it from the fire of 1871, and would undoubtedly have rescued it once more had he been in town. Unfortunately he was absent from the city and this valuable collection of books was lost. It contained some volumes of rarity and age which cannot be replaced. The labors of a lifetime spent in collecting what was rare and valuable in literature were wasted in a single night. What is Mr. Scammon's loss is that of the city also, and there will not be lacking thousands of cultivated people in Chicago to lament with him the catastrophe which destroyed his precious collection of books.

RECOVERY

1874 – 1888

(THE officers of the Historical Society, with at least $60,000 in prospect from the Gilpin Estate, decide that the time has come to revive the organization. The first meeting in more than three years takes place on November 17, 1874, in the Club Room of the Tremont House. The minute book contains the following record.

There were present and answering to their names the following members, to wit:

HENRY A. JOHNSON	B. W. RAYMOND
JULIAN S. RUMSEY	LUCIAN TILTON
SAMUEL JOHNSTON	PERRY H. SMITH
E. T. WATKINS	GEORGE L. DUNLAP
MAHLON D. OGDEN	GEORGE F. RUMSEY
EDWARD BURLING	SAML. H. KERFOOT
GEORGE M. BOGUE	JOHN N. JEWETT
J. Y. SCAMMON	L. B. BOOMER
ARTHUR H. BURLEY	E. W. BLATCHFORD
GEORGE H. ROZET	THOMAS H. ELLIS
JOHN B. CALHOUN	N. B. KIDDER
JOSEPH S. REED	JOHN H. DUNHAM
EDWIN H. SHELDON	BELDEN F. CULVER

The President reported concerning the financial condition of the Society as follows:

"The President, in connection with Mr. George F. Rumsey, a member of the Executive Committee, sold the iron, brick and stone remaining in the ruins of the Library building after the fire, and received therefor $2908.83, and also collected from . . . . Mr. J. Y. Scammon on account of funds of the Society in his hands $3475, making $6383.83. Out of this the President has paid on account of the mortgage debt of the Society, held by Mr. Mark Kimball, Receiver, $4000 of principal for which bonds were received and cancelled, and $1405.01 on account of interest on said mortgage, also $676.80 for sundry items including special assessments and taxes. The Society holds a certificate of deposit of the Marine Company, Savings Department, dated Sept. 23rd, 1873, for $13,949.60 drawing interest at 10% pr. annum from January 1st, 1874, on account of the Endowment Fund."

. . . . The Hon. J. Y. Scammon presented a catalogue of the Society's collections which had been made subsequent to the great fire of October, 1871, and which were afterwards destroyed by the fire of July 1874. The portraits of General Grant and of Miss Snead and a few books and pamphlets were saved from this latter fire. . . . .

The next step is an appeal for funds. The appeal takes the form of a printed circular, undated but issued some time in 1876.

CHICAGO HISTORICAL SOCIETY

The Executive Committee of this Society, deeming that the time has come for a renewal of active work, makes the following statement:

The Society has thirty-two thousand dollars in Chicago

city bonds, and expects to receive the still further sum of about thirty thousand dollars, all constituting the proceeds of the Gilpin bequest, but which, by the terms of the will, must be held for the period of ten years, at and not before the expiration of which time the principal and accumulations thereon can be used.

The Society owns the lot on the northwest corner of Dearborn avenue and Ontario street, valued at twenty thousand dollars, which is still encumbered to the amount of about nine thousand dollars, being part of an original loan made by the Society.

The Society has a claim against the Savings Department of the Marine Bank, amounting to about seventeen thousand dollars, which is in process of collection; and the Committee is assured and believes that this claim will be secured and made available as far as required for the payment of the debt on the lot, leaving the balance for other purposes.

Notwithstanding the above encouraging statement, the Society has no available means for present uses.

It is proposed to erect on the said lot, in the early spring, a brick building, of suitable dimensions, so located as not to interfere with the erection hereafter of a permanent structure, and also to employ a Secretary and Librarian to conduct the active operations of the Society. To do this and to provide for contingent necessities, the sum of Eight Thousand Dollars will at once be required.

Since the fire of October, 1871, or for the past five years, the subscriptions of three hundred dollars each, previously paid by Life Members, have been yielding the Society interest at the rate of ten per cent or thirty dollars yearly; while the Annual Members, whose yearly dues were twenty-five dollars, have paid nothing. It is a difficult matter to determine what would be a fair and just assessment to make on the members under such circumstances; but the Committee has decided to ask the Annual Members to submit to an assessment of Fifty Dollars each for the entire interregnum of five years, with a hope that many will deem it a privilege to increase that amount; and they also ask the Life Members to contribute as their liberality, ability and knowledge of the needs of the Society may dictate.

The Committee is of the opinion that in this way a sum of at least eight thousand dollars can be raised, which, with the annual dues hereafter to be collected, will place the Society in a position to resume its former activity and usefulness, and they feel assured that abundant material is at the command of the Society that can, by proper effort, be secured to give importance and attractiveness to its collections, and which will continue to increase in value as time advances. The Society's active existence re-established, its members and friends will once more have furnished them the opportunity for those pleasant reunions which were so marked a feature in its former days of prosperity.

The Committee, moreover, feels fully justified in making and urging this appeal on the ground of the dignity, usefulness and importance of its objects and purposes, not only as touching the present benefit to arise from its work but as regards the good to accrue to posterity.

Isaac N. Arnold,	Edwin H. Sheldon,
Geo. F. Rumsey,	Mark Skinner,
Julius Rosenthal,	Levi Z. Leiter,
E. T. Watkins,	John De Koven,
George L. Dunlap,	*Executive Committee*

⟪ *The Society proceeds with its plans. The officers let the contract for a small building to be erected on the Society's lot at Dearborn and Ontario streets, and employ Albert D. Hager, whose career comprised experience as farmer, teacher, geologist, pisciculturist, and superintendent of the Washingtonian Home for reformed drunkards, as Secretary and Librarian. Mr. Hager takes a long chance on salary: he agrees to work "at such compensation as may be hereafter determined by the Executive Committee and in the judgment of said Committee the means of the Society will warrant."*

One of the new Secretary's first duties is the collecting of the fifty-dollar assessment levied on annual members. He keeps a straight-faced memorandum of his experiences. His assignment, difficult at best, is made almost impossible by a railroad strike which, in early July, destroyed much property and caused great apprehension among businessmen.

The Book of Records will show that it was decided to erect a building on the lots of the Society at the N.W. corner of Ontario & Dearborn sts. The contract for the erection of the building was awarded to John McEwen who agreed to do all the work and find all the material (with privilege of using the old brick and stone as far as they would answer the purpose) for the sum of $2429. This did not include the safe door, which will cost about $100. Eight men subscribed each $250 and this subscription with the addition of $125 raised by Mr. Arnold elsewhere, was the entire amount of funds available except such as might be had of the members for assessments and initiation fees due. I was requested to make the collection of the assessments—or annual dues of the members—which, by a vote of the Executive Committee, was fixed at Fifty Dollars each for the entire five years that had elapsed since the fire of '71.

On the 4th of August, I started out to make the collection. First called at Williams & Thompson's office to get their assessments. Norman Williams was east—would not be back till September. Thompson not in office—would be in a day or two. Called at Isham & Lincoln's. Both gone east. Will be back Sept. 1st. Called at Sanford E. Loring's office. Was out of his office, getting ready to go east on Monday next. Called on Genl. Stockton. Was too much cramped for money to pay anything now but taxes and the necessaries of life. Thinks well of the Society—glad it is being started and only regrets that he is not able now to do something for it. The Riots have had the effect to stop dividends on his R.R. stock.

W. W. Chandler, the newly initiated member, said he was very badly off—the rioters having destroyed property of the Line in which he had a large interest to such an amount that instead of dividends there might be assessments on the stockholders. He said his line—the Red Star Line—had lost 105 locomotives and cars enough, if placed in line on the road with locomotives attached, to make 18 miles in length of cars & engines that had been destroyed by the rioters. Many of the cars were filled with freight for which the company was responsible. He said he must have a little breathing spell before he could give any check. Chas. Hitchcock was in his office. Said that inasmuch as he had never been called upon for assessment had about concluded some one had kindly made him a life member. Hesitated about giving a check. Said he "would see" and write me and probably would send check.

Edward Goodman was out of town—would be back next Thursday. He sends the *Standard* regularly.

Perry Smith says he paid $500 toward the building that was burned and he thinks that should constitute him a Life Member—and therefore declined paying any assessment.

E. T. Watkins out of town: will be back in a week.

L. B. Boomer was not in office, but at Poughkeepsie, N. Y. I wrote him a letter.

H. H. Magie was in Paris, I also wrote him a letter.

Wm. Hickling was out of office—gone home.

E. W. Jones was out of town—would be back in a few days.

F. G. Welch ditto.

J. V. Le Moyne says he has not the money to spare now, but may have it by & by. Likes the Society and will furnish more Cong. Docs. for our Library.

H. G. Miller out of town.

S. T. Atwater not in office.

August 6

R. S. Critchell gave check for $25.

Lyman Blair thinks he cannot spare the money—had rather lose all he has paid than pay any more.

E. W. Jones says he don't belong to the Society & never did.

Wm. Hickling—not in office.

F. G. Welch—not in office.

S. B. Chase gave check for $50.

W. D. Kerfoot out of town—will be back in a few days, perhaps tomorrow.

S. T. Atwater—says he is too poor to pay anything— even books.

August 7

H. N. Rust will probably give books—cannot give money.

William C. Dow—says he is too poor to give either books or money.

C. P. Kellogg says trade is dull he don't feel able to give—is obliged to turn worthy people away every day because he has not the money to spare. Likes the Society and if trade revives in fall will give his check for $50.00.

H. W. King was evidently a little out of humor for he did not seem at all pleased to form my acquaintance and said he did not know as he should accept the membership (he said in his reply, "I accept") but would see Mr. Arnold, and motioned the next man, who was waiting, to see him, to come in. He had evidently been *begged* so much that he was getting tired of it.

Aug. 8–11

Alfred Cowles of the Tribune said he had more calls for money than he had the ability to answer as he would like. Thought it a "very inopportune time" to build a Hall for the Society. He had more worthy and pressing calls for money than ours and therefore should not give anything now and did not know if he ever would. If times improved he might do so, but would not promise to.

Frank R. Chandler gave check for $25 and may conclude to become a Life Member—and if not may give the other $25.00.

George E. Stanton is out of business and in consequence of the depreciation of real estate is now too poor to do anything, and as long as the Secty. of Treasury continues to burn and "retire" money and thus cripple him in common with all others who own real estate he could not pay a dollar, but if they stopped "retiring" & times were good again he might give something.

L. C. P. Freer had never attended any meetings, but if he was obliged to pay supposed he should pay—would not promise ever to give a dollar.

Geo. M. Higgingson says he is too poor to pay—wishes he was able, for he thinks well of the Society and would like to give something to help revive it and will if he can get some books for us.

J. Rosenthal says he cannot spare the money now—will pay as soon as he is able. Thinks well of the Society—will give books and did give two—one published about 235 years ago and Carrington's "Battles of the American Revolution," a nice book.

Geo. W. Smith was east—will be back Sept. 10th.

S. B. Eaton lives in New York—wrote him, 346 Broadway.

S. C. Griggs says his health is poor and he is not able to give money but will try and give books. Wants to remain in the Soc.

Dr. H. A. Johnson was not in office.

E. H. Sargeant says he is not a member of the Society— has interest in it and if times were better would give something for its support.

August 9th

John H. Dunham says he guesses he is not a member *now*. After talking awhile he said, "When I get $50 I will think of the Society"—but would not promise.

Eli Bates was not at 250 So. Water St. but had moved to 82 Beach St.

Geo. M. High says he cannot do anything now. Would like to help if he could.

A. H. Burley out of town. Had talk with his son. He thought his father would not give.

Pretty poor show for so many calls—only $200. This I paid over to the Treasurer, Mr. Smith.

Mr. Hager also notes the day-to-day progress of the building, and works off his own frustrations by recording them.

On Monday the 12th day of August 1877 the first stone for the foundation of the new building was laid. On the Monday following, the foundation had been finished and the floor timbers were laid. On the 19th day of Aug. the floor timbers were put on and door frames placed.

On the 26th the ceiling timbers were, in part, put in place. On the 31st the roofing was done and furrings for the lath were being put up, and the masons took away their scaffolding &c to another job. The Cox Brothers did the brick work and are to do the plastering. On Saturday the 8th Sept. the rough coat of plastering was done. Mr. Geo. F. Rumsey made a payment of $1000 towards the building to the contractor, John McEwen. He was obliged to advance some, I think, out of his own pocket. I collected $250 of E. H. Sheldon and $250 of L. Z. Leiter. Mr. Rumsey is not well—has very sore eyes—but still it appears as though he and Mr. Arnold, the Prest., were the only *working* men on the Executive Committee. They work well. Sept. 12th Mr. Arnold & Mr. J. S. Waterman of Sycamore, Ill., called. The latter voluntarily gave his check for $100 to be applied toward the new building. The coarse plastering is drying—not dry yet. I am having a colored man (Johnson) clear off the old brick, rubbish &c putting them into the low places and covering them with dirt, preparatory to fitting up the vacant spaces for a flower garden & yard.

Sept. 15th, Saturday. During this week no work has been done by the contractor. The rough coat of plastering is dry. The tuck pointing has been commenced. Johnson, the colored man whom I hired, has finished clearing the dirt out of the basement.

Oct. 13, '77. This day we moved the books from 44 Ashland Block into the new building which is completed. I have had six double book cases made for $200.00 by Mr. John McEwen the contractor. Into these I put most of the books.

Oct. 16. Had gas fixtures put into the building today. Mr. E. Bagot furnished the side lights and Mr. H. W. Witworth furnished the two drops or chandeliers free. In the evening was held the first meeting of the Soc. in the new building.

Oct. 20. The building is not quite paid for and Mr. McEwen is provoked because he has not got his pay. Mr. Geo. F. Rumsey the active man on the Building Committee is confined to a dark room with sore eyes and is therefore unable to make the collections necessary to "square up" for the building.

Nov. 8, '77. This day have finished placing the Wis. Hist. Soc. contribution of books upon the shelves. Mr. McEwen called and could not realize why I should be willing to work here without any pay except what may be allowed me by & by and the pay that results in the consciousness of doing some good in the world and building up a good and much needed institution that will secure and preserve the history of important and interesting times in which we live. He has evidently no sympathy with such work. Instead of aiding he seems to prefer to hinder its progress. He made six book cases as before remarked and made them as he says according to the specifications, with six shelves in height in each. By placing seven shelves in each, as I have, twenty-four more shelves are needed to fill the cases.

I told him I wanted very much to have those shelves so that I could fill the case before our annual meeting on the 20th and proposed to pay him extra for them—would pay him $5.00 where he said it was worth only $3.00 to do the job. His reply was, "I am not working for money on this job. I am working for glory. If you will get me the money due from Rumsey on this job I will do the job for nothing, but if you don't I will not do it for $10.00. And I will make the platform too when that is paid, but not before."

I tried to explain to him that I had not the power to make Mr. R. pay or not pay him, and could not see the exact justice there was in punishing me because others were derelict in duty. I had paid him for the cases as I agreed & did it too before he had finished doing what he acknowledged was for him to do. If there is glory or honor in doing this I say with profound reverence Good Lord deliver me from such honor or glory.

⟦ *The new building might be small, unpretentious, and temporary, but it was the Society's own, and a matter of pride. The* Tribune *describes the first meeting in the new structure, held on October 16, 1877.*

The Chicago Historical Society held its first meeting in its new and decidedly cozy-looking little building, corner of Dearborn avenue and Ontario street, last evening. The Hon. I. N. Arnold, President of the Society, occupied the chair, and a very fair attendance was present.

After the reading and approval of the minutes, the President congratulated the members of the Society on the fact that they were once more gathered in a building of their own—a building which, while of a temporary character, was only an earnest of what was to come. Not the least gratifying feature in connection with the enterprise was that the building was substantially paid for, thanks to the contributions of several public-spirited citizens. . . . . It was only within the last few months that an attempt had been made to revive

---

CHICAGO HISTORICAL SOCIETY.

A quarterly meeting of the Chicago Historical Society will be held in the

NEW HALL OF THE SOCIETY,

North-west corner of Dearborn and Ontario Streets, on Tuesday Evening, the 16th inst., at half past seven, sharp. You are invited. Several interesting papers will be read.

CHICAGO, October 13th, 1877

Albert D. Hager,
Secretary.

---

the Society. The result of these efforts was shown in this building, and a few hundred volumes towards a library. Here was the beginning of what he hoped would grow to be something worthy of this great city. Mr. Arnold then dwelt upon the needs of Chicago and the entire absence of public libraries, and said:

". . . . If Chicago, already so eminent in many things, aspires to become also a literary centre, and to irradiate the great valley of which she is the commercial representative, she must foster with liberal aid and generous appreciation her literary institutions; more, she must encourage and honor men of culture, letters, and science.

"Her merchant princes must learn that while it is something to build an elevator, to make a harbor, to open a canal, to construct a railroad, it is also something equally honorable, at least, to found a library, to establish a college, a university, or a school of learning.

"No one doubts that our citizens have the bold enterprise, the sleepless activity, the earnestness, the energy which will enable them to make the most of their material advantages, but no wise citizen will be satisfied with this. It is time for Chicago to aim at a generous emulation with her sisters in the arts, in taste, in letters, in all those pursuits which give grace, elevation, and dignity to the human intellect and character.

"Chicago must not follow Carthage, or Venice, or Liverpool, or Amsterdam, alone, as models; let her learn, also, from Alexandria, Athens, and Florence. . . . .

"We have boasted long enough of our grain-elevators, our railroads, our trade in wheat and lumber, our business palaces; let us now have libraries, galleries of art, scientific museums, noble architecture, and public parks, specimens of landscape gardening, and a local literature; otherwise there is danger that Chicago will become merely a place where ambitious young men will come to make money and achieve a fortune, and then go elsewhere to enjoy it. You must have culture, taste, beauty, art, literature, or there is danger that our city will become a town of mere traders and money-getters; rude, unlettered, hard, sharp, and grasping. Let us sow the seed generously, and, even if we do not ourselves live to gather the fruit, those who shall hereafter reap the harvest will bless the sowers. . . . ."*

The President then offered some resolutions of thanks to Mrs. Gordon, James S. Waterman of Sycamore, Gen. Buckner, D. W. Mitchell, the Andrews Atlas Company, the Pennsylvania Historical Society, and others for contributions of articles, atlases, works for consultation, etc., for the use of the Society. The resolutions were adopted.

The President also offered resolutions requesting Mrs. Newberry and Mrs. W. B. Ogden to furnish portraits of their late husbands, former Presidents of the Society. The resolutions were adopted. Judge Skinner offered a similar resolution in reference to Mr. W. H. Brown, also a former President of the Society. The resolution was adopted.

On motion of the President, Gen. W. E. Strong was elected a member of the Society.

The Hon. William Bross read . . . . an interesting and valuable paper . . . . on Col. J. W. Foster. . . . .

The President announced that a brief paper had been prepared by Mr. Barnes on the location of the true site of

---

* See pp. 47–48.

Father Marquette's grave, and, in accordance with the President's invitation, Mr. Barnes gave a brief account of his visit to the grave at St. Ignace, on the site of old Fort Mackinaw, last month.

The President also announced that a paper had been prepared by one of the best known members of the Society on two of the most distinguished Indian Chiefs of the Northwest—Billy Caldwell and Shabonee. As the author desired to make some additions, however, it had been thought best to defer the reading of the paper until the next meeting. It was also announced that, at the annual meeting on the 20th of November, Bishop Clarkson, of Nebraska, would read a paper in commemoration of the Hon. William B. Ogden.

The Secretary, Mr. A. D. Hager, read an exhaustive paper on the excavations in the mounds of Whiteside County, near Sterling. The Society then adjourned.

(*The* Tribune, *of course, carries other local news in the same issue—October 17, 1877—in which the Society's first meeting in its new building was reported.*

GOV. NICHOLLS, OF LOUISIANA

Gov. Nicholls, of Louisiana, is in the city. Yesterday he went on 'Change, and was introduced to many of the mercantile magnates, upon whom he made a favorable impression by his genial manners and pleasant conversation. He warmly supports President Hayes' policy of pacification and obliteration of the color line in Southern politics. He thinks there will be peace and harmony hereafter between the races in his State, and he intends to contribute all in his power to that end.

⟨ *The devastated North Side, taken soon after the fire of 1871.
Looking south along and to the east of Pine Street, now North Michigan
Avenue. The picture was probably taken from the Water Tower,
which withstood the flames.*

PROCLAMATION

WHEREAS, In the Providence of God, to whose will we humbly submit, a terrible calamity has befallen our city, which demands of us our best efforts for the preservation of order and the relief of the suffering, be it known that the faith and credit of the City of Chicago is hereby pledged for the necessary expenses for the relief of the suffering.

Public order will be preserved. The police and special police now being appointed will be responsible for the maintainance of the peace, and the protection of property.

All officers and men of the Fire Department and Health Department will act as Special Policemen without further notice.

The Mayor and Comptroller will give vouchers for all supplies furnished by the different Relief Committees.

The headquarters of the City Government will be at the Congregational Church, corner of West Washington and Ann streets.

All persons are warned against any act tending to endanger property. Persons caught in any depredation will be immediately arrested.

With the help of God, order and peace and private property shall be preserved.

The City Government and the committees of citizens pledge themselves to the community to protect them, and prepare the way for a restoration of public and private welfare.

It is believed the fire has spent its force and all will soon be well.

R. B. MASON, Mayor.

GEO. TAYLOR, Comptroller. (By R. B. Mason.)
CHAS. C. P. HOLDEN, President Common Council.
T. B. BROWN, President Board of Police.

❨ *October 9, 1871:
"Whereas, In the Providence
of God . . . a terrible calamity
has befallen our city. . . . ."
At left, Samuel Stone,
Assistant Librarian,
the last person to leave
the Society's building
on October 9.*

⟨ *A hymnal, "The Spirit of Prayer," was the only book from the Society's library to survive the fire. Below, what remained of the Society's "fireproof" building after the fire.*

⟨ *Mrs. Henry D. Gilpin and Henry D. Gilpin.*
At a critical time, the Gilpin bequest saved the Society.

⟨ Healy's "Honora Sneyd,"
saved from the fire of 1874,
destroyed by the fire of 1954.

⟨ The Tremont House, Lake and
Dearborn streets, where the Society
was reorganized in 1874.

❲ *The only extant picture of the Society's "temporary building" (1877–1892), Dearborn and Ontario streets.*

❲ *The Fort Dearborn Memorial tablet, 1881, with Robert J. Bennett of W. M. Hoyt & Company.*

THIS BUILDING OCCUPIES THE SITE OF OLD FORT DEARBORN, WHICH EXTENDED A LITTLE ACROSS MICH. AVE. AND SOMEWHAT INTO THE RIVER AS IT NOW IS.
THE FORT WAS BUILT IN 1803 & 4, FORMING OUR OUTMOST DEFENSE.
BY ORDER OF GEN. HULL IT WAS EVACUATED AUG. 15, 1812, AFTER ITS STORES AND PROVISIONS HAD BEEN DISTRIBUTED AMONG THE INDIANS. VERY SOON AFTER, THE INDIANS ATTACKED AND MASSACRED ABOUT FIFTY OF THE TROOPS AND A NUMBER OF CITIZENS, INCLUDING WOMEN AND CHILDREN AND NEXT DAY, BURNED THE FORT.
IN 1816 IT WAS RE-BUILT, BUT AFTER THE BLACK-HAWK WAR IT WENT INTO GRADUAL DISUSE AND MAY 1837 WAS ABANDONED BY THE ARMY, BUT WAS OCCUPIED BY VARIOUS GOVERNMENT OFFICERS TILL 1857 WHEN IT WAS TORN DOWN, EXCEPTING A SINGLE BUILDING, WHICH STOOD UPON THIS SITE TILL THE GREAT FIRE OF OCT. 9, 1871.
AT THE SUGGESTION OF THE CHICAGO HISTORICAL SOCIETY THIS TABLET WAS ERECTED BY
NOV. 1880.   W. M. HOYT.

❨ *John Wentworth, in the Society, as everywhere, a center*
of controversy, and Albert D. Hager, Secretary, 1877–1887.

Chicago Historical Society.

The regular quarterly meeting of the Society will be held at its rooms, 142 Dearborn Avenue, at 8 o'clock, on

Tuesday Evening, July 21, 1891.

Maj. JOSEPH KIRKLAND will read a paper on " The Bones of John Lalime," illustrated with the supposed relics them-selves.

JOHN MOSES,

Chicago, July 16, 1891.   Secretary.

❡ *Invitation to "one of the most enjoyable midsummer meetings" the Society ever held. Below, Lalime's bones as they are today.*

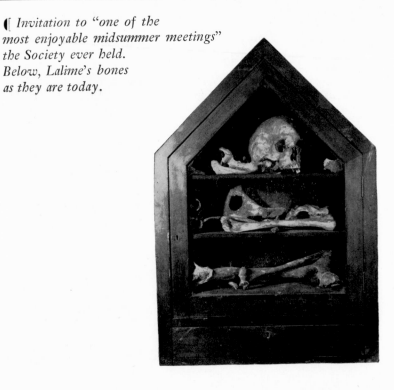

RECEPTION TO HON. E. B. WASHBURNE

The reception tendered last evening by the citizens of Galena to the Hon. Elihu B. Washburne on the occasion of his return to their midst as a private citizen after a protracted public career of distinguished usefulness and honor, was a demonstration remarkable alike for its heartiness and for its non-partisan character. It was a Galena affair, in which politics had no part. Old friends and neighbors, Democrats as well as Republicans, improved the opportunity to testify their affection and esteem for a man who has honored his city, his state, and his nation.

BASE BALL - FINIS, THE END

To chronicle the last game of the season between League clubs on Chicago ground is an easy task—made more easy by press of other matter, which abbreviates this. Chicago beat Boston by heavy hitting, luckily put in and backed by horribly bad play by Brown, of the champion team. Reis closed the season in a blaze of glory, having been hit only six times up to the last inning, which was played in the dusk. Eggler's fast and clever running, Anson's hard hitting, Reis' well-judged pitching, and Brown's awfully loose catching were the features of the game.

RUNS SCORED

Innings—	1	2	3	4	5	6	7	
CHICAGO	5	1	0	6	0	1	2 —	15
BOSTON	0	2	0	1	2	0	2 —	7

GEN. JAMES SHIELDS

Gen. James Shields, who served as a Brigadier General in the Mexican War, and was shot through the body in one of the battles, who represented the State of Illinois six years in the Senate of the United States, and represented Minnesota a term in the same body, who served in the War of the Rebellion, and is now a venerable citizen of Missouri, will deliver a lecture in this city, at McCormick Hall, on Oct. 30, before the Catholic Library Society. His subject will be "Reminiscences of the Mexican War."

❡ *The Society's building committee—George F. Rumsey and George L. Dunlap—winds up its work by submitting a report to the Executive Committee when that committee meets on December 11, 1877.*

The Building Committee appointed by the Executive Committee of the Society respectfully report:

That immediately after their appointments, they made efforts to secure funds by subscription for the erection of the building then contemplated and for which plans had been procured, but it became painfully evident that those plans must be abandoned for want of funds. As the directions to the Committee were to erect such building as they could procure funds for, which might answer the needs of the Society, another plan was procured and the present building is the result.

The Committee felt that it was vital to the life of the Society that a comfortable room of its own should be secured, and feel that they have succeeded in securing one which will answer for some years with comfort and security and may at any time be incorporated in a larger building or added to for appearance or additional room.

The entire cost of the building was $2755.50, and subscriptions have been received amounting to $2520.25 and

there is due to settle all the bills the sum of $235.25.
Subscribers:

J. T. RYERSON	25–	MARK SKINNER	250–
E. T. WATKINS	100–	J. S. WATERMAN	100–
E. H. SHELDON	250–	S. M. NICKERSON	250–
G. L. DUNLAP	250–	C. B. FARWELL	85–
L. Z. LEITER	250–	W. B. OGDEN	250–
JOHN CRERAR	250–	G. F. RUMSEY	100–
W. S. JOHNSON	250–	J. S. RUMSEY	100–

[*Parenthetical account, in the Minutes, by Albert D. Hager:*
"The *mania* among contractors for 'extras' (amounting to
'steals' of thousands of dollars in many of the county and city
contracts during the last few years) did not seriously affect
the cost of this building. Its interests were closely watched
by the Executive & Building Committees."]

❡ *An ardent Southern Illinois member of the Society—lawyer, legislator, and long-time friend of Abraham Lincoln—
asks the Secretary's pardon for an excess of zeal.*

EDWARDSVILLE 7th April 1879

FRIEND HAGER,

You are a very wicked man. By means of your blandish-
ments I have been stirred up to such unwonted zeal in getting
up old letters, documents, &c, for your Society that I have
fractured several Sabbaths—so much so that I am afraid that
I have done as Mr. Lincoln said Ben Wade told him he had
done. Wade said to Lincoln: "Mr. Lincoln, during the administration of Mr. Buckhannon I prayed to Almighty God
that he would lengthen out the life of Chief Justice Taney
during the administration, but I'll be G—d d— — — —d if

Historical Society Rooms,

Chicago, January, 1878.

We are happy to announce that the Chicago Historical Society is again in active operation, and has a new building of its own, corner Dearborn and Ontario Streets, which we hope may prove a safe one We wish to collect and preserve in its library every thing that relates to the history of this country, and more especially of Chicago, Illinois, and the north-west.

We also desire, as far as possible, to preserve for future generations the history of the world to-day. To accomplish this, we respectfully ask for contributions of historical, statistical and scientific books; newspapers, old files, as well as those now being issued; Indian and mound builders' relics; well authenticated accounts of the Indians and first settlers; sketches of the lives of eminent persons who have lived in the state; the signification of the Indian names of rivers, lakes, etc. We particularly desire to secure official reports; national, state, municipal, religious, literary and scientific. We desire full sets of these, and in order to get them we ask each one who may read this, to look over his old books and papers, and if among them he finds any annual reports of city or state officials; catalogues of schools; pamphlets containing any statistical information; or any book, pamphlet, magazine or directory published in Chicago before the fire, we earnestly ask that it may be presented and preserved in the library of the society for future reference.

Autograph letters of distinguished men of the present and past, specimens in the departments of natural history, paintings and statuary are also very acceptable and will be properly cared for.

Isaac N. Arnold, Pres't.

Albert D. Hager, Sec'y.

I don't believe I have overdone the thing!" Now I am afraid that I have overdone it, and if I have, you are to blame for urging me doing *thusly*. I have been gathering up all sorts of trash—newspapers, maps, old letters, the Lord knows what all. If I have been loading you down with worthless rubbish pardon me, for it was under many tribulations and misgivings that I made up my mind to send this last package. If I have egregiously erred remember me in your prayers.

Yours in fraternal bonds,

J. GILLESPIE

¶ With fitting ceremony the Society marks the site of Fort Dearborn at what is now Wacker Drive and Michigan Avenue. The report is that of Albert D. Hager, Secretary.

In pursuance of notice previously given, the President and members of this Society convened, on the 21st day of May, 1881, at the wholesale grocery House of W. M. Hoyt & Co., corner of River Street and Michigan Avenue, to unveil a memorial tablet of Old Fort Dearborn which the senior member of that firm, in response to an invitation from H. N. Rust and other members of this Society, had placed in the wall of his storehouse. The tablet is of Vermont marble. In the upper panel is a *bas relief* view of the old Block House. In the lower panel is a suitable inscription giving a brief history of the old Fort.

President Arnold called the meeting to order. The buildings in the vicinity were richly decorated with flags and oil paintings representing views of the Old Fort. Eight companies of the First Regt. I. N. G. preceded by a band of music took position near the platform on which were many of

Chicago's early settlers and honored citizens. A large concourse of people filled the streets. After the President had stated the object of the ceremonies a prayer was offered by Rev. Jeremiah Porter who preached the first sermon in the old fort, forty-eight years ago. Mr. R. J. Bennett of the firm, W. M. Hoyt and Co., in a suitable speech made a formal presentation of the tablet.

Col. Gurdon S. Hubbard, the earliest settler of Chicago now living, drew aside the Union flag that covered the tablet. The audience loudly cheered and the band played Hail Columbia. Hon. Thomas Hoyne responded to the presentation speech of Mr. Bennett, after which Mr. Eugene J. Hall of Lawndale read an appropriate poem. Hon. John Wentworth was then introduced and read a valuable historical paper relating to the old fort and the people of its time. A valuable map of Fort Dearborn reservation on which was located the boundaries of the Old Fort, the Light House, &c., was presented to the Society by the venerable Alexander Woolcott, the county surveyor.

This concluded the exercises of the occasion. It is proper to state that Mr. W. M. Hoyt generously paid the whole expense incurred in placing the beautiful tablet in its site and for manufacturing the same. The thanks of this Society are justly due to Mr. Hoyt. Posterity will hold his name in grateful remembrance for having so appropriately marked the ancient site of Old Fort Dearborn.

◖ *John Wentworth, for the Society, proposes a policy governing the use of its collections which has prevailed to this day. The first paragraph comes from the minutes of a meeting held on October 18, 1881; Wentworth's resolution was adopt-*

ed at the annual meeting held on the following November 15.

Even without special consideration A. T. Andreas turned out the three-volume History of Chicago *which continues to be the most valuable single source of information about the city.*

[October 18, 1881]

The secretary . . . . suggested the desirableness of having an exhaustive and authentic history of Chicago written and published under the auspices and direction of this Society and gave notice that a gentleman—Capt. A. T. Andreas—was willing to undertake the work and bear the entire expense, provided the Society would extend to him the full use of its library for consultation and its leading and best informed members would coöperate with him in his efforts to make a thoroughly reliable history and one in every way worthy of such a historical city as Chicago: Hon. Wm. Bross expressed himself in favor of the proposition and moved that a committee of five be appointed of which President Arnold should be chairman to confer with Capt. Andreas and report the result at a subsequent meeting. The motion was carried and Messrs. Arnold, Bross, Hoyne, Hager & Sheldon were appointed.

[November 15, 1881]

Mr. Wentworth arose and introduced the following resolution, which after some discussion was adopted, viz:

"Resolved that the committee appointed at the last meeting to consult with reference to a history of Cook County, or of Chicago, be discharged from the further consideration of the subject. And that this Society welcomes to a free use of its library all writers and publishers of history and all persons in any way interested in historical pursuits; but it

111

deems it inexpedient to lend its influence to one person in preference to another, or to become in any way responsible for the use of facts in its possession to which all persons are equally welcome."

❡ *Robert Lincoln, unimpressed with the historical importance of his father's papers, demurs to a proposal that he turn them over to the Chicago Historical Society. The "few" papers, when opened to the public at the Library of Congress in 1947, make up 194 bound volumes, and constitute a body of incomparably valuable source material.*

WAR DEPARTMENT
WASHINGTON. Aug. 27th, 1882.

Albert D. Hager, Esq.,
DEAR SIR:

In reply to your letter of August 7th respecting the custody of letters and documents received and preserved by my father and mother, I have to say to you that the idea of placing them in the custody of the Historical Society would strike me with favor if there was anything of sufficient consequence to include in such a collection. I have not examined any of my mother's papers, and do not believe that anything will be found among them of sufficient importance for preservation. The papers left by my father were few in number, and have been for some years in the custody of Mr. Nicolay, who is, with Col. Hay, engaged in preparing a biography.

Mr. Nicolay is now out of town, and I have not been able to confer with him on the subject; but I will take an opportunity of doing so when he returns.

Very truly yours,
ROBERT T. LINCOLN

❴ *By publishing George Flower's* History of the English Settlement in Edwards County, Illinois, *the Society makes an
outstanding contribution to the history of the state. The
Librarian, breaking all rules, had allowed a member to with-
draw the manuscript a few days before the fire of 1871; thus
it escaped destruction. The story of the publication is told
in an exchange of letters and a note in the minutes of the
Executive Committee for November 11, 1882.*

Hon. Isaac N. Arnold
President of the Chicago Historical Society
DEAR SIR:

Twenty-two years ago there was presented to our Society a manuscript History of the English Settlement in
Edwards County in this state from its commencement in 1817
by Morris Birkbeck and George Flower. From a cursory
examination of it myself, and what is said of it by those who
have carefully read it, I am satisfied it is a valuable contribution to the history of our state.

It is replete with incidents in the lives of Gov. Edward
Coles, Morris Birkbeck, Richard Flower, and others of that
noble band who fought out the battle of freedom in our state
in 1823–4. In the interest of the history of the state, and in
justice to the memory of Mr. Flower, who so generously
presented it to the Society, I think it should be published.

I will cheerfully defray the expenses.

Yours very truly,

L. Z. LEITER

CHICAGO,
Aug. 30, 1882

L. Z. Leiter, Esq.

DEAR SIR:

I have received your note of the 30th of August, authorizing the publication at your expense of the History of the English Settlement, in 1817, of Edwards County, by Morris Birkbeck and George Flower. For this act of liberality, and appreciation of a valuable and extremely interesting contribution to the history of our State, you are entitled to the thanks, not only of our Society, but of all lovers and students of history. Your generosity enables us to publish a manuscript which would long ago have been given to the public, had not the means and resources of this Society, been crippled by the great fire of 1871.

I desire to add to the thanks of the Society, my own not only for this liberal act, but for the example which I hope and believe, will be the beginning of a series of contributions through the agency of our Society, to the history of our State, and the North-West.

Very truly yours,
ISAAC N. ARNOLD
President of the Chicago Historical Society

[Nov. 11, 1882]

The President announced that since the last meeting of the Society a volume of about 400 pages—the History of Edwards County—had been brought out. Mr. Leiter had paid the expense and Mr. Washburne had edited the work. By a vote of the Committee the Librarian was directed to furnish each member of the Society with a copy and it was suggested that he have copies in readiness to give to all the members who should attend the Annual Meeting. On motion of Mr. Wentworth the price of the book was fixed at 3.00 a copy and the Sect was instructed to take charge of the sales and keep a record of the same.

◀ *Secretary Hager, disdaining the round-about approach, makes a frontal attack on a prospective donor. He gets his money. There are still books in the Society's collection whose bindings are credited to Mrs. Meacham.*

CHICAGO, June 16, 1883

Mrs. Eliza Meacham
New Haven, Vt.
DEAR MADAM,

Yesterday I called upon Dr. Calvin Wheeler with the hope of getting him to give this Society $300 or $500 to be expended in the binding of pamphlets and newspapers which the Society now has on hand and which *should* be bound and preserved. . . . . But the Dr. had been called upon for money so many times of late, that he positively declined giving the sum asked for and I left. . . . .

And now I am going to "pop a question." I beg you don't be alarmed. If you say "No, I thank you," I will be like the "other fellow" who was refused when he proposed to marry a girl. He replied to her "No" by saying in a self-satisfied manner, "Well, you are not the *first* one that has said NO to me." And so I say. Dr. Wheeler said "No" and possibly you will, and possibly you *ought* to say "No." I know very little of your *financial* standing. If you have not an abundance of this world's goods to take you comfortably through it, I say by all means say *no, no,* a thousand times NO. But if you have $300 to $500 that you can safely spare

I ask you to give it to this Society for the specific purpose of binding up such historical books as we may have that need binding, that they may make glad the hearts of those who may come after we have gone to our reward. It is a duty which we owe to posterity to preserve the history of today for them. Your sister, Mrs. Wheeler, was in favor of her husband's giving the money called for.

It is a little curious that this Society is indebted more to women than to men for its success. The will of Mr. Gilpin was defective, and *by law* this Society could not have recovered a cent of the property. But the widow, Mrs. Gilpin, insisted that the Society should have it and consequently today has over $57,000 of the "Gilpin Fund." Lucretia Pond of Petersham, Mass., gave the Society its other fund of

> To the generosity of MRS. ELIZA
> MEACHAM, of New Haven, Vermont,
> The CHICAGO HISTORICAL SOCIETY
> is indebted for the binding of this book.
> CHICAGO, November, 1883.

$13,500. Indeed, all we have in the way of funds was given by *women*. Mrs. William Hicklin came to the rooms a few months ago, before we thought of having the papers bound, and said she wanted to be an Honorary Life Member & gave her check for $500. Will you be the second lady on that list? If you can, consistently, I hope you will. If you do not, I shall call upon another lady to do so. I hope you will give me an early answer. Upon the inside of each cover will be noted the fact that you paid for the binding of that book.

Your name will last longer and be read with more gratitude and respect in all coming time than if it were placed on the handsomest and most durable stone monument ever made. $500 is cheap for *such* a monument, to say nothing of the satisfaction that results from the consciousness of having done a good deed for humanity. Will you have the *enduring monument* made? Pardon me for writing this long and badly written letter and believe me

Faithfully Your Friend,
A. D. HAGER

(*The Society takes official notice of the death, on January 17, 1885, of its founder.*

A quarterly meeting of the Society was held in its hall January 20, 1885, President Washburne in the chair. . . . .

Judge Skinner submitted the following resolutions which were approved:

Resolved, That the Chicago Historical Society, in the death of the Rev. William Barry, deceased, mourns the death of its original founder, its first Secretary and Librarian, its earliest and best friend and the one to whose zeal and enthusiasm, above that of all others, it owes its early and great success, as well as its establishment of a permanent foundation.

A profound student of history, a good scholar, an accomplished writer, a courtly and elegant gentleman, a good business man, possessed of great good judgment, remarkable tact, and untiring industry, he accomplished, for this Society, at its outset and during the first years of its existence, results equally surprising and satisfactory, and which secured to the Society a most respectable position amongst kindred associations, not only in this country but in foreign lands, the benefits of which are enjoyed by our Society at the present time, and give us a name and place that but for his efforts could hardly have been attained even at the present time.

Judge Skinner further moved that the family relatives of the late Rev. Mr. Barry be requested to present to the Society a portrait of founder Barry, which was unanimously agreed to.

❴ *A reporter for the Chicago* Herald *wanders into the Chicago Historical Society, and sketches its Secretary for posterity. The article appeared in the* Herald *for June 20, 1886.*

SHADOWS OF THE PAST

Not a great ways north of the river, on Dearborn Avenue, stands a queer old brick building of one high story, severely plain in exterior, rather uninviting, and, on the whole, cheap and cheerless. The gorgeous green stone apartment house next door seems a palace in comparison, but whoever walks that way and fails to pause a moment for a peep inside will miss something worth even a busy Chicagoan's while. For in this queer old building are more queer old things than the wayfaring man ever supposed were to be found in all Chicago.

Just within the door the visitor will meet one of the queerest and quaintest specimens in the collection—a round-headed, white-haired old man, whose face is sure to wear a smile of welcome that would warm the heart of a money-loaner, and whose graciousness could not fail to charm the most indifferent into ease and expectancy. His name is Hager, and he is the Secretary of the Chicago Historical Society, whose home this old building is.

The secretary is just like the building wherein he spends the days from early morn till late at night—plain and unpretentious outside, rich within, redolent of reminiscence, a storehouse of the past, a cyclopedia of the rare, quaint and ancient. He is at once a librarian, a historian, a geologist, antiquarian, ethnologist, genealogist, biographer, archaeologist, bibliographer, enthusiast. His devotion to method is only equaled by his industry, and his infallible memory is matched by his perennial humor. What he does not know about the history of Chicago and the men who made it is not worth knowing. The tittle-tattle about men and things of bygone days which he has not on his tongue's end would make but a short and dull story. Not one of the subjects of his discourse was ever more interestingly loquacious than himself, and in his office as connecting link between past and present he throws a glamour of romance over commonplaces which a more prosaic commentator would mention only with wearisomeness.

If nature in all her works ever made a man especially and wholly to fill the functions of secretary of a historical society she made him when she grew and ripened this quaint and lovable old man. His treasures are those which every citizen of Chicago should regard as his own with the public's —treasures rich enough to be without a duplicate in all the world, and precious enough to be worthy a safer and more fitting repository. In this plain and insecure old building are hundreds of thousands of articles and volumes relating to local and general history, many of which, lost, could never be replaced. Their care-taker knows where every one of them is, to the most inconsequential pamphlet or relic. There are copious indexes made with great labor and renewed with care, but the best index is that lodged in the secretary's white head.

With great pride the historical enthusiast exhibits the interesting articles in his collection. . . . .

"There, sir, is a razor with which one of the greatest men that ever lived was shaved. I mean George Washington. It was exhibited at the Centennial. This razor was sixty-five years in Judge Gillespie's family, by whom it was always treated as a sacred relic. There is no doubt that it was Washington's razor, as it was given to one of Judge Gillespie's ancestors by an inmate of Washington's family. Here is a lancet with which the Father of His County was bled. It comes from a Mrs. Lewis, whose grandfather Tyndall was a revolutionary soldier, attached to Washington's staff, and picked up the instrument just after a camp surgeon had used it in bringing blood from the veins of the Commander-in-Chief. . . . .

"On the wall there hangs the first map of Chicago village, made by James Thompson in August, 1830. By its side is the original manuscript of Mayor Mason's famous fire proclamation, which was heard around the world, presented by Luther Laflin Mills. That old picture of Fort Dearborn, showing the big locust tree and the Lake House, hung for several years in the barroom of Mark Beaubien's hotel, the Sauganash. Here is a section of a black oak tree found recently in a bed of clay eight feet below the surface at the corner of Halsted street and Belden avenue, its surface plainly showing the effects of the action of the waves, and indicating that the shore of the lake was once that far to the west. We have——"

But at this point the secretary's daily dinner of bread and milk made its appearance in the willing hands of a grand-daughter, and the enumeration of the society's treasures was temporarily interrupted. Between spoonfuls of milk the round-headed old enthusiast informed his guest that scarcely a beginning had been made at the work of "taking in" the collection, and promised that there were hundreds of other beauties to be unfolded.

Yet there are many thousands of people in Chicago who have never heard of this quaint old building and its rich stores, and whose hearts were never made lighter by brief converse with the white-headed secretary. Need the *Herald* add that admission is free to all and that the fare to Ontario by Mr. Yerkes' street cars is but a nickel?

([*John Wentworth, often a center of controversy, becomes the object of a row between the Executive Committee and the Chairman of the Committee on Nominations. Mr. Kerfoot took his own prerogatives so seriously that he printed his objections in a four-page folder which he sent to the Society's entire membership.*

A paragraph in the minutes of the Executive Committee meeting held on September 20, 1886, records the incident which gave rise to the dispute.

Mr. Wentworth called the attention of the committee to the fact that his name was not in the list of Honorary Life Memberships in the printed List of Members, and asked that the Executive Committee direct the Secretary to place it there, as he had subscribed $500 for the building in 1867 as shown upon the subscription book. The committee declined doing as requested, but instructed the Secretary to notify the committee on nominations that it was the wish of the Ex. Com. that Mr. Wentworth's name be presented and recommended for Honorary Life Membership at the next meeting of the Soc.

CHICAGO, October 16, 1886

Mr. A. D. Hager,
Secretary of the Chicago Historical Society.

DEAR SIR: In answer to your communication addressed to me, dated the 15th instant, allow me to say:

First. Perfectly ready, as I am at all times, to assume any necessary responsibility in any position which I may occupy, or in which I may find myself placed, I do not feel that such urgent necessity exists for my instant individual action in the matter named by you, as to justify me in taking any such step without consultation with, and the concurrent action of the other members of the Committee on Nominations to membership in the Chicago Historical Society.

Second. If, as, however, I do not think to be true, Mr. Wentworth is now, BY VIRTUE OF THE PAYMENT OF A SPECIFIC SUM OF MONEY, either entitled to the place, or DE FACTO an occupant of the position of Honorary Life Membership, and if the supreme power in the Historical Society, to wit: the Executive Committee has so decided, then no nomination of Mr. Wentworth, and no customary reference of such nomination to this Committee, and hence no scrutiny, or examination or endorsement of such nomination by this committee are at all necessary.

Third. The Committee on Nominations can entertain and act upon the question of fitness and desirableness of nominees for membership of any grade only upon the usual, and so far invariably observed, method of nominations made VIVA VOCE or by formal written communication by some member, and heard read or made in open meeting of the Society.

Fourth. I do not deem that it falls within the province or scope of the duties or powers of the Committee on Nominations to determine such questions as are now presented to it as the basis of its actions, and as are involved in the history of Mr. Wentworth's contribution of money to specific funds for specific purposes and NOT, at the time, made by him as an express admission fee to any grade of membership in the Historical Society.

Fifth. Were I called upon, and were it necessary or proper for me individually or singly to decide the question now apparently placed before our committee, and to act as any committee-man on nominations ought to act, namely, on the evidence laid before it and him, I would say that if Mr. Wentworth, in 1867, was elected an Honorary member of the Society at a meeting PREVIOUS to his making the subscription or contribution to the fund for building purposes, then he certainly had already become an Honorary member before the time of, and not in consequence or by reason of that subscription or contribution; and the money having, at that time, been given, received and used for a then nominated purpose, no EX POST FACTO application of that money could or can properly be made to secure for him any grade or quality of membership.

Sixth. I think that it is without precedent that the Executive Committee has ordered or requested the Committee on Nominations to report, favorably or unfavorably, upon the name of any person as that of an individual worthy or unworthy of membership of any kind, grade or character, and hence, I doubt the ability of that Executive Committee in 1886, to determine that, by reason of an amendment made to the constitution in 1883, MONEY unconditionally and unqualifiedly, by any bargain, paid into the treasury of the Society in 1867, can now, at this late date, be applied, by them or the donor thereof, to the purchase of honor, place or position in the Society—such honor, place or position not having been in existence or contemplated to, afterward, exist when that mere money was so paid into that treasury.

Force is given to this by the fact that Mr. Wentworth, at the time of his donation, prescribed the use to be made of it.

For the foregoing reasons I, as an individual member of the Committee of Nominations am constrained to decline to report the name of Mr. Wentworth as that of a gentleman to be, in 1886, ELECTED to Honorary Life Membership of the Chicago Historical Society, on the ground of his having, in 1867, paid into its treasury for a purpose by him then indicated, the sum of five hundred dollars.

Such a step on the part of the Society would open the tomb, resurrect, revive and give uncontemplated efficacy to many other contributions long since made and used for the purpose then prescribed by the contributors, and which use then so made has long ago rendered the money FUNCTUS OFFICIO, and hence now powerless for any new or other use or purpose.

It is just to myself as well as to Mr. Wentworth, that I should add: There may be many other and good grounds (with which, however, I am unacquainted), upon which Mr. Wentworth should be honored farther than he has been by the Society; but, upon the one named in your letter to me, I am clear that he should not be advanced to any higher plane than that upon which he now stands in the association.

If that plane be, as it now appears to be, simply that of Honorary Membership, which does not give him, and never has given him, the right to vote or hold office—and Mr. Went-

worth now stands before the Society as never to have possessed the necessary qualifications entitling him to the honors
and privileges which the Society has heretofore deemed him
capable of receiving—all this is no fault of, or question before,
the Executive or this Committee.

In conclusion, I venture to suggest that if the gate to
an Honorary Life Membership is now open to Mr. Wentworth, and the condition precedent to his entering that membership is the payment of five hundred dollars to the Society,
then the problem presented to him is easy of solution, and his
check, of the present date, payable to the order of the treasurer
of the Society for that amount, is all that he need give or do
to gain admittance; for, doubtless, the Committee on Nominations would then, and on that ground, approve of the name
of Mr. Wentworth, when presented according to rule, as
that of a gentleman admissible to the grade of Honorary
Life Membership in the Chicago Historical Society.

Respectfully, etc.

S. H. KERFOOT,

Chairman, etc.

❲ *Secretary Hager talks up to E. G. Mason, newly elected
President of the Society.*

CHICAGO HISTORICAL SOCIETY

140–42 DEARBORN AVENUE

CHICAGO, ILLINOIS, 11/26, 1887

E. G. Mason, Esq.

DEAR SIR,

In closing your letter to me of the 21st you say "trust-
ing that all disagreements are at an end, and that the affairs

of the society will now proceed harmoniously" &c. I don't understand what you mean. I made you a proposition in my letter of the 16th to retire from the society upon the doing of certain things upon your part. You did not agree to it. It was all dependent upon the action of the Executive Committee. There has been no meeting of the Executive Committee since a year ago last September and I see no better prospect in the future than there was in the past for a meeting. *It is too uncertain.*

Since I wrote you, I have seen and talked with several of the members and received letters from others, and invariably I am requested to remain in the Society. I have a letter from a gentleman who has "remembered" the Society in his will—and who subscribed $1000 towards the new building who writes: "The Society needs you much more than you need it and I beg that you will stand *unflinchingly* for the Society's sake rather than your own," &c. In an interview with Dr. Pearsons he seemed almost on the point of giving up all his interest in the Society and declared that if I was *kicked out* he would not give a cent towards the new building or have anything more to do with the Society. He is too valuable a man to be turned out, as he says, by "exchanging a man who has worked faithfully and *successfully* for the Society ten years, for Judge (?) Moses" who has had no library experience and is not known by half the members of the Society. You know, Mr. Mason, that this library is of unprecedented growth. There is not, and never was, a historical society, ten years of age, that had so good a library and so well arranged as this. I have asked you, in the kindest terms, to tell me what my faults are—why those men who rarely if ever visit these rooms, are so anxious to turn me out? I will esteem it a favor if you will tell me. I will try and do better, if I am told in what respects I do wrong. I have done the best I could—and those who know me best, & know about the library, are my best friends. These are the ones that desire me to stay and I have agreed that I will stay and in the future do as well as I have done in the past—provided I am elected. I am therefore a candidate for re-election.

If your suggestion that "all disagreements are at an end" means that I am *out* of the Society, I think you may be mistaken, for I shall not go out voluntarily, at present. But if you feel like letting "bygones be bygones" and start your administration with a desire to work for the Society's good and permit me to do so, without hindrance, I shall be as glad to have "disagreement" at an end as you—and will do my best to have the Society "proceed harmoniously."

Knowing as I did the treachery of Mr. Kerfoot, and of his unpopularity, I hated terribly to have him elected to an official position—but as he is *in*, I shall not make a "row" even if he *abuses me*, as he has in the past; and nothing but his attack upon the Society will make me utter a word of disapproval.

My friend Pearsons has proved himself to be what I have said to you, a man who took a delight in doing good and would give us generous assistance in case we should erect a new building. Out of the $8,500 which I said was pledged for a new building, $5,000 was from him. He keeps his promises—but he said if I was out, he would not give *one cent;* for the Society would go down, and would need no new building. Mr. S. T. Atwater of Buffalo, visited the Rooms about three weeks ago, and spent some time in looking at the collections—especially the "Atwater Collection" which he deposited here in 1878, which was bequeathed to the Society by his wife. He was well pleased at the arrangement I had made of his wife's contribution and suggested that we ought to have a *better* and *safer* building in which to keep our valuable library. I asked what he would give towards one. He said: "I am old—over 80—not long to live and have made my will and given away my property to my relatives, but if you will build a house *before I die*, I will give $1,000 towards it." I told him we would try, at which he expressed a wish that we would. So you will see that we have $9,500 pledged towards the *beginning* of a building which I hope will be built during your administration. God grant that it may be so!

If I am elected, I may not be able to attend personally to the library *all* the time during the *coldest* weather, for this room cannot be made warm and my lungs are very tender; but I will have a faithful man visit the rooms daily, and attend to the mail and packages that may be sent here.

I hope you will see that the wishes of the two daughters of the late Philo Carpenter be gratified by having the money which he bequeathed ($1000) used to pay for the binding of books and his name, upon a card, be placed on the inside of the cover of each book, bound and paid for with his money. I introduced a resolution at the meeting in Oct. to this effect, but Mr. Kerfoot opposed it, and thus exhausted the treasury of the general fund, and, if I had entered it upon the records —which I did not—would have been a lasting disgrace to the Society—to refuse the request of the heirs of the only man in Chicago who has bequeathed any *money* to the Society during the last ten years.

Now, Mr. Mason, do you want to wipe out old scores and begin and work with me as that dear good man, your predecessor, did? If so, I beg you to say so, and you will find me

Your friend,

A. D. HAGER

In a lifetime of learning Hager had missed one fundamental fact: in a contest with the boss, the hired man has no chance.

The Executive Committee met on December 6, 1887.

The meeting was called to order by the President, E. G. Mason.

Albert D. Hager having resigned from the office of Secretary and Librarian, the following resolution offered by Henry J. Willing, was unanimously adopted.

Resolved, That the Chicago Historical Society upon the retirement of Professor Albert D. Hager from the office of Secretary and Librarian which he has filled for the past ten years desires to express to him its full appreciation of the industry and fidelity which he has displayed in the collection and care of its library, and its cordial thanks for all that he has done to conserve and advance the interests of the Society; and that in token thereof the Society recommends to the executive committee that a sum equivalent to the salary heretofore paid to the Secretary and Librarian for a period of three months shall be paid to Albert D. Hager in equal monthly instalments commencing on January 1st, 1888.

Thereupon the Society proceeded to vote by ballot for a Secretary and Librarian which resulted in the election of John Moses—he receiving 22 votes to 5 cast for Albert D. Hager and one for Charles Harpel.

EXPANSION

1888 – 1896

(THE Executive Committee decides that the time has come for a new building, and appoints a sub-committee, consisting of E. G. Mason, H. J. Willing, and D. K. Pearsons, to formulate plans for raising money. The sub-committee reports on March 1, 1888.

The sub-committee appointed Dec. 6, 1887 to report a plan for securing a fund with which to erect a building for the uses of this Society, with suggestions of the amount which can be raised and usefully employed for this purpose, made a report recommending the appointment of a committee authorized to solicit subscriptions for a fund to be employed for the erection of such a building, and suggesting that the amount of one hundred and fifty thousand dollars can be raised and usefully employed for this purpose.

On motion of G. W. Smith, seconded by Henry J. Willing, it was unanimously resolved that the whole executive committee be constituted a subscription committee each member of which shall be authorized to solicit subscriptions for a fund not exceeding one hundred and fifty thousand dollars to be paid to and held in trust by the Chicago Historical Society to be employed solely for the erection of a building for the uses of this Society on its property at the north west corner of Dearborn Avenue and Ontario Street, and that such subscriptions shall be payable and subject to the call of the Executive Committee when the sum of seventy-five (75) thousand dollars is subscribed for this purpose, and that the President of the Society be authorized to have prepared and to furnish to each member of the Executive Committee a book containing the proper form of such subscription.

It was also unanimously resolved, that L. Z. Leiter and E. G. Mason be authorized to obtain from competent architects sketches and preliminary plans of a suitable building for the purpose aforesaid, upon the express understanding that the services of such architect or architects shall be limited to this preliminary work only; and that no architect shall be otherwise employed until the further action of the Executive Committee.

❲ *A popular author entertains the members of the Society at the regular quarterly meeting on July 16, 1889.*

. . . . The president then introduced Mrs. Mary Hartwell Catherwood, who read two chapters from her forthcoming romance, "The Story of Tonty." The first, the scene of which was laid in Montreal, describes the meeting of La Salle with Jeanne le Ber; the last entitled "The Undespairing Norman," contains an account of the effect upon Tonty of the news of the assassination of La Salle, and the apparition of the latter to his faithful lieutenant at Starved Rock. The audience, composed largely of ladies, listened with breathless attention, being fascinated alike by the absorbing interest of the narrative, the grace and polish of its diction, and the pleasing voice and manner of the reader. On motion of Gen. McClurg, the thanks of the Society were tendered

Mrs. Catherwood for the rare literary treat which she had afforded the members and invited guests.

And the meeting adjourned.

JOHN MOSES, *Secretary.*

(*At a regular quarterly meeting on July 21, 1891, the Society receives a bizarre addition to its collection, and the members enjoy a pleasant evening.*

. . . . Maj. Joseph Kirkland has enriched our department of local historical relics in the presentation of the supposed skeleton of John Lalime, which forms the subject of his paper tonight.

Major Kirkland was . . . . introduced by the President, and entertained a delighted audience with a clear and ample statement of all known circumstances connected with the killing of John Lalime, "the little Frenchman," by John Kinzie, the first American resident of Chicago, in a personal encounter.

At the close of the reading, Fernando Jones, a resident of Chicago since 1835, made some interesting remarks on the question of identification, confirming the conclusion that the skeleton presented to the Society was that of John Lalime.

President Mason added that it was the presentation, discussion, and preservation of papers like this, relating to the early history of our great city, which explained and justified the existence and value of the Society.

On motion of Gen. A. C. McClurg, the thanks of the Society were tendered Major Kirkland for his valuable historic paper, with the request that he deposit a copy among its archives for future reference.

On motion adjourned.

After the adjournment, some time was passed inspecting the supposed remains, and in pleasant conversation by the many old settlers and visitors present upon topics relating to early Chicago history, making this the most enjoyable midsummer meeting the Society has held for years.

JOHN MOSES, *Secretary*.

❲ *Raising money for a new building turns out to be a slow and arduous process, but a bequest of $25,000 from John Crerar, and an accumulation of more than $50,000 in the Gilpin Fund, assure success. The contract is let on October 13, 1892. Two weeks later, on November 12, President Mason lays the cornerstone. The* Tribune *describes the ceremonies.*

Two hundred persons assembled at the northeast corner of Dearborn Avenue and Ontario Street at 3 o'clock yesterday afternoon to witness the laying of the cornerstone of the new building of the Chicago Historical Society. . . . . The derrick that was to hoist the stone was gaily decorated with flags. . . . . As the air was unpleasantly chilly the ceremonies began promptly on time by E. G. Mason, the President of the Society, calling on the Rev. Dr. R. W. Patterson to offer prayer. After the prayer Mr. Mason delivered an address covering the work accomplished by the organization. He said [in part]:

"This structure will be in all respects the finest historical society building in this country. Its total cost when completed and fully equipped will be $150,000, of which $125,000 has been provided, and we believe we can rely upon this community to furnish the remainder. Some of our benefactors are among those of the incorporators who have passed away. Others deserving special mention are Henry D. Gilpin, the most generous contributor to the society funds; John Crerar, whose beneficence has blessed almost every good institution in Chicago; and Edwin H. Sheldon, the devoted friend of the Society and its ready helper in time of need. Nor should I fail to speak of that efficient and honored President of the Society, Isaac N. Arnold, who gave so much time and labor to its welfare; nor of his successor, the distinguished statesman, Elihu B. Washburne, who was the first to edit and publish volumes of the Society's collections.

"To them and to other friends whose munificent gifts have made it possible to rear the structure of which we lay the cornerstone today we return praise and thanks. But we know that to each of them it will be an all-sufficient reward if we place here a building truly consecrated to the high objects of this Society, in which shall be gathered the memorials of the origin and growth of this wonderful city and this marvellous Northwest, and the materials for their history free to all who may desire to consult or study them.

"It is to be the home of an institution not for the advantage or under the control of any sect or clique, but designed to benefit the whole community in which we dwell. This is ideal, and the laying of this cornerstone today marks a long step towards its accomplishment."

Mr. Mason then introduced the Rev. Dr. F. M. Bristol, who delivered an eloquent address on historical institutions and research. . . . . .

Judge John Moses, the Secretary of the Society, then read the list of articles which were deposited in the iron receptacle in the cornerstone. . . . . The masons then spread cement under the stone, and lowered it into its place, after which Mr. Mason spread a layer of cement over the top of the box, and declared the cornerstone duly laid. . . . .

. The new building, designed by Henry Ives Cobb, will be one of the handsomest in the city. It will be of granite, Romanesque style. Its general ground dimensions are 120 feet on Dearborn Avenue by 100 feet on Ontario Street, but there is a court at the northwest corner. It will be only two stories and a basement in height, but its steep roofs make its greatest height eighty feet. . . . . The material used is Wisconsin rock-faced red granite for the fronts, and steel for the interior. It is designed to be as completely fireproof as possible. . . . .

The roll of the officers of the Chicago Historical Society from its beginning reads like a list of the pioneers and celebrities of Chicago. The first President, William H. Brown, who served until 1861, was succeeded by Walter L. Newberry, who served until he died in 1868. The next President was J. Y. Scammon, who resigned in 1870, and was succeeded by Edwin H. Sheldon, who in 1876 gave way to Isaac N. Arnold. E. B. Washburne, who was elected in 1884, served three years and was succeeded by the present incumbent, E. G. Mason.

❲ *Other news items reflect the concerns of the nation's second city, now a metropolis of 1,100,000 inhabitants.*

JAM IN THE STREET

A yawning trench, four feet deep and from six to eight feet wide, at State and Madison streets, for the west side cable line loop, caused an immense amount of inconvenience to people and teams yesterday at the most crowded corner in Chicago. The trench extended north on the west side of State Street for half a block and crowded all the immense volume of vehicular traffic over upon the east side of the street. All day long the teams floundered in the congested area, and at the four corners of Madison and State the four policemen had their hands full in straightening out the blockades that happened every half hour and in piloting people who became bewildered or faint to places of safety.

CAPTURED TWENTY PICKPOCKETS

Every officer available at the Central Station was detailed last night during the Democratic procession to look out for pickpockets. As a result, before midnight twenty notorious thieves were packed into cells in the basement of the City Hall.

AT FIVE O'CLOCK TEA

Mrs. Lyon and Mrs. Conger, No. 262 Michigan Avenue, gave a tea yesterday afternoon at 5 o'clock. They were assisted in receiving by Miss Hodgeman, Mrs. Hickox of New Orleans, Mrs. W. B. Howard, and Mrs. Charles Hamill. At the table in the dining room were Mrs. Charles Deering, Mrs. Hugh McBirney, Miss McAvoy, and Miss Wadsworth.

ROOM FOR EDUCATORS

At its meeting next Wednesday the Executive Committee of the World's Fair will determine whether or not the Educational Building shall be erected. . . . . Several weeks ago the question of providing room for the Educational Building was referred to Director of Works Burnham for an estimate of the cost of a structure affording 150,000 square feet of exhibit space. Mr. Burnham has turned in no report and no plans have been matured. . . . .

Said one director: "It looks absurd for the Board of Directors to provide forty acres of space for bulls, rams, horses, and hogs and yet refuse a modest appropriation of $150,000 for an Educational Building. I trust the Executive Committee will be shamed into doing its duty."

LAKE FOREST BEATEN

Northwestern University took first place in the race for the Northwestern College League pennant yesterday by defeating Lake Forest University by a score of 18 to 0.

The contest took place at Athletic Park in Lake Forest. Fifteen hundred people witnessed the game, with enough of the fair sex to put the players on their mettle.

⟨ *The Executive Committee, mindful of the fire of 1871, decides to take no chances in the new building.*

The Chairman reported [on April 11, 1893] that the cost of the new building of the Historical Society, according to the present contract and estimates, would be $142,800, the whole of which sum had been provided except $5,050. That to make the whole building absolutely fireproof, so that there should be no combustible material in it, according to the estimates of the architect would cost $26,000 additional. On motion of D. K. Pearsons seconded by G. W. Smith it was unanimously

Resolved: That the new building of the Chicago Historical Society be made absolutely fireproof, and so as to contain no combustible material, according to the plans and estimates of Henry Ives Cobb, Architect, at an additional cost not exceeding Twenty Six Thousand Dollars; and that the chairman of the building committee be authorized to make the necessary contracts therefor.

❲ *Members attending the annual meeting held on November 17, 1896 at the University Club learn that one of their number refuses to be abolished.*

. . . . The President, as chairman of the Executive Committee, then reported that committee's recommendation of the following gentlemen for membership in the Society, to wit:

Life Members:—Richard T. Crane, who has contributed $1000 to the building fund of the Society, and Belden F. Culver, who has rendered services and made contributions to the Society exceeding in their value the regular $500 dues of life members.

Honorary Members:—Samuel D. Ward, who is the only survivor of the original board of officers of the Society, and who is one of its three surviving incorporators.

Annual Members:—Thomas D. Jones, David B. Jones, John N. Jewett, Charles H. Starkweather, Frank H. Starkweather, Charles F. Quincy, Frank P. Schmitt, J. Lewis Cochran, John A. Spoor, Lewis H. Boutell, H. H. Kohlsaat, John P. Wilson, and E. J. Gardiner.

On motion of Mr. Goodspeed, duly seconded, the Secretary *pro tem* was authorized and instructed to cast the ballot of the Society for the gentlemen whose names had been so reported for their election as such members. The Secretary thereupon cast the ballot as instructed, and the President declared the said gentlemen duly elected.

Daniel Goodwin then asked the President what had become of the associate members of the Society, to which the President replied, that class of membership had been abolished by the new constitution, but notwithstanding that fact, Mrs. M. M. Donoghue refused to be abolished, and insisted upon paying, regularly, her annual dues of $10 as such member, and that hence she now constituted the entire associate membership of the Society.

(*On December 15, 1896, the Society proudly opens its new building to members and their guests. The* Inter Ocean *describes the dedicatory meeting.*

The Chicago Historical Society was "at home" to its friends last night in its new and beautiful home at the corner of Dearborn avenue and Ontario street.

From 8 until 11 o'clock several hundred invited guests reveled in the beauties of the building and its treasures of historic interest, listened to interesting addresses concerning the Chicago Historical Society, and enjoyed a collation served informally in the subbasement.

As the guests entered the main hall they were received by the officers of the society and their wives, as follows:

Messrs. and Mesdames—Edward G. Mason, A. C. McClurg, Edward E. Ayer, Lyman J. Gage, George W. Smith, Henry J. Willing, Daniel Goodwin.

The reception committee stood before the massive fireplace, formed of stones from the Illinois Central depot and the Cook County courthouse after the great fire of 1871, and from the Nixon building, the latter being the only one in the business district which survived the conflagration of a quarter

The Chicago Historical Society

invites you to attend the

exercises at the opening of its

New Building

on Tuesday evening, December the fifteenth,

eighteen hundred and ninety six,

at eight o'clock.

142 Dearborn Avenue.

Please reply.

of a century ago. From dome to basement the building was brilliantly illuminated with electricity and decorated profusely with palms, garlands of smilax, and potted plants.

Throughout the evening the sweet strains of an orchestra hidden in a bower of palms floated through the building, except the lecture-room. In this beautiful portion of the structure nearly 500 guests gathered at 9 o'clock and listened with interest and appreciation to addresses regarding the past, present, and future of the Chicago Historical Society. . . . .

President Edward G. Mason and Dr. N. S. Davis describe the founding of the Society and its forty-year uphill struggle. Of greater interest is the address of former Congressman George E. Adams, who foresees that the Society will grow as the city grows.

. . . . The Historical Society in the career of larger usefulness which I believe is open to it will be sure of the material support of Chicago business men. I infer this, not from the past and present of the Historical Society, but from the past and present of Chicago. What a wonderful history our city has had! We have done here in sixty years the work of several generations. That work has been mainly material. We have been laying the material foundations for the city of the future. How proud we have been of our city; but the pride of Chicago people in Chicago for many years was hardly more than vanity. We were vain of the bigness of our city and its rapid growth, but for a generation past our pride has been assuming a soberer view. Our pride in our city is colored with a sense of responsibility. The business men of Chicago feel that, as its material greatness has been due largely to what they have done in the past, so its moral, social, and intellectual greatness will depend on them hereafter. They are resolved that it shall be something more than a great city of industry. We know what many of them have done for music, for art, for science up to this time, we know that they have resolved that it shall be a fitting place of abode for cultivated men and women, as well as a great center of industry, so that we may be assured that whatever support is necessary to make the future of the Historical Society what it ought to be will not be lacking.

Now, ladies and gentlemen, what should it be? What do we wish it to be? If you or I had the power by our wishes expressed tonight to fix the character of this institution twenty years hence, what would our wishes be? We could not wish for a more beautiful building. We might wish, and we do earnestly wish, for a larger collection. We hope the collection of books and valuable papers will grow to fill the utmost capacity of the present building. We hope it will outgrow the building, and then we hope for a larger building to contain the larger collection. But that is not all.

We want the Historical Society to be not merely a valuable and interesting collection, housed in a beautiful building; we want the administration of this collection to be such that it shall be useful as well as interesting. We want it to be to the very largest extent accessible to the public. We want the public not only invited but attracted to visit it and to stay. . . . .

Think what influence the intellectual life of this great city is likely to have on the intellectual life of the nation. What the American national character of the twentieth century will be we can only faintly discern. That it will be strong and original, I have no doubt. That it will differ widely from the New England and Virginia type of fifty years ago, I am convinced. We who are children of Englishmen who settled the Atlantic coast 250 years ago may have been taught to consider the American as a seventeenth-century Englishman slightly modified by a new environment. We may think that what we call the sturdy Anglo-Saxon type of national character will assimilate all new elements of population without being greatly changed. How can we be sure of that? Do we not know that the Englishman of Queen Elizabeth's time, the

145

noblest national figure of modern history, poet, philosopher, warrior, explorer, and lawmaker, was himself the result of a combination of nearly the same elements of national life and thought and feeling which for the last fifty years have been combining here to produce the typical American of the twentieth century?

. . . . It took hundreds of years in England to reach this grand result. Here in our electric and stimulating air and with our habits and facilities of travel it may be reached within a generation. When the New Englander and the Virginian, and the Celt, the German and the Scandinavian, who helped to make the old-world Englishman, have fully acted and reacted on each other, and each has had his due influence upon American thought and feeling, then will come the blooming time of American art and literature, then will come our Elizabethan age.

And where is it that these varied influences most strongly and harmoniously work toward this result? Whether we wish it or not, whether it accords with our sense of the fitness of things or not, it is here at the greatest railway center of the United States. Chicago is destined to be the typical city of the American people. It is not with pride, it is rather with a solemn sense of responsibility that we ought to feel that what the artistic and intellectual life of Chicago will be a generation hence the intellectual and artistic life of America is destined to become.

May it not have been through a conscious or unconscious prevision of this that the businessmen of Chicago have already done so much for the future of their city in founding libraries and museums and art institutes and other institutions of learning? Is it not to this end that the founders and supporters of the Chicago Historical Society have labored? If the future of this Society is to be full of beneficent influence on the intellectual life of this great city and the whole American people will it not be largely due to the wise and disinterested zeal of those who have made its past and present secure?

QUIET

PROGRESS

1896 – 1927

NEW building, new rules and regulations. The Executive Committee, meeting on December 18, 1896, adopts a code.

. . . . The following Regulations concerning the use of the Society's collections were adopted:

1. The Museum and Halls of the Society will be open to the public on Monday and Thursday of each week from 9 A.M. to 5 P.M.

2. The Building of the Society shall on all secular days be open to Members, and those introduced by any of the Officers, or approved by the Secretary at the Building. (Subject to the right of the Executive Committee to close the doors of the Building at any time for reasons satisfactory to itself.)

3. No person may consult or examine any book or manuscript belonging to the Society except a Member, a Donor, or one introduced by one of the Officers or approved by the Secretary at the Building.

4. No book or other article shall at any time be lent to any person to be removed from the Building except by express consent of the Executive Committee.

5. All manuscripts of the Society shall be kept under lock and key, and be used only in the presence of the President, Librarian, or his assistant.

6. No paper or manuscript read before the Society and deposited therewith shall be published except by consent of the author and of the Executive Committee.

7. No manuscript, and no part of a manuscript, belonging to the Society shall be copied, except by permission of the Executive Committee, after an application in writing specifying the manuscript or part thereof desired to be copied; and if any manuscript belonging to the Society shall, in consequence of such permission, be published, in whole or in part, the fact that it was obtained from the Society shall be required to be stated in its publication. But this provision shall not be construed to prevent the publication of names, dates, and other chronological memoranda, without special permission.

8. The use of tobacco, and conduct not consistent with the quiet and orderly use of the Library and Reading Room are prohibited.

(In 1896 the Society employed, as Secretary and Librarian, Charles Evans, who had served in responsible positions at the Boston Athenaeum, the Indianapolis Public Library, the Enoch Pratt Free Library in Baltimore, the Omaha Public Library, and the Newberry Library, and had just finished organizing the Virginia Library of the McCormick Theological Seminary. For reasons now forgotten, Mr. Evans and the Executive Committee fail to get along together. With unusual brusqueness the Committee discharges a distinguished librarian who would, a few years hence, make a monumental contribution to scholarship in the form of his American Bibliography.

The minutes of the same Executive Committee meeting— November 25, 1901—that record the dismissal of Evans note

(*The Gilpin Library of the Chicago Historical Society
as it appeared about 1906. Below, the Society's building, 1896–1932.
The structure still stands at Dearborn and Ontario streets.*

(*Fernando Jones, Honorary Member, in Indian costume.*
He liked to write verse.

(*Invitation to the Theodore Roosevelt meeting, December 8, 1908.*

The Chicago Historical Society
requests the honor of your presence
at a Reception
in the Society's Building
Dearborn Avenue and Ontario Street
Tuesday evening, December the eighth
nineteen hundred and eight
at eight o'clock
on the occasion of the
presentation of a portrait from life
of

Hon. Theodore Roosevelt
President of the United States
by A. Benziger
A gift to the Society from Mr. Henry C. Lytton
Presentation address
by
Rev. Frank W. Gunsaulus

《 Portrait of Theodore Roosevelt,
Honorary Member of the Chicago Historical Society,
presented by Henry C. Lytton in 1908.

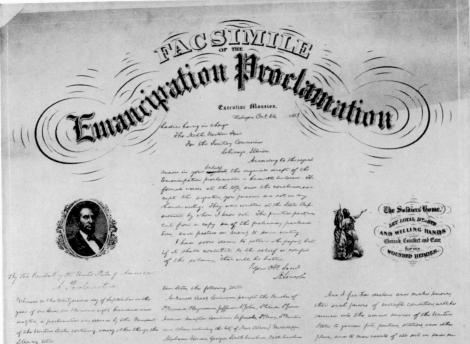

Lithographed facsimile of Lincoln's Proclamation of Emancipation, January 1, 1863. The original, placed in the Society's building for safekeeping, was destroyed in the Great Fire of 1871.

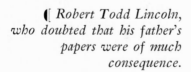

1809 - 1909
The Chicago Historical Society
requests the honor of your presence
in the Society's Building
Dearborn Avenue and Ontario Street
Friday evening, February the Twelfth
nineteen hundred and nine
at eight o'clock
at exercises commemorative of the
One Hundredth Anniversary
of the birth of
Abraham Lincoln
Colonel Clark E. Carr, of Galesburg
will deliver an address entitled
"Lincoln at Gettysburg"

❲ *Invitation to the
Society's Lincoln Centennial
meeting, February 12, 1909.*

❲ *Robert Todd Lincoln,
who doubted that his father's
papers were of much
consequence.*

⁅ *The Fort Dearborn Centennial exercises, 1912, on the terrace of the George M. Pullman home, Prairie Avenue and Eighteenth Street.*

⁅ *Stephen A. Douglas Centenary exercises at the Douglas Monument. Bishop Charles Edward Cheney speaking, with gestures.*

*❙ Martin F. Douglas and Miss Caroline McIlvaine, the Society's
Librarian, at the Douglas Centenary exercises.*

⟨ *An Old Settlers' Meeting at the Society, October 9, 1913.*

⟨ *A case of Civil War relics*
in the Society's museum.
About the year 1915.

the employment of a successor who would serve the Society devotedly for a quarter of a century.

. . . . The following resolutions were offered by Mr. Bowen and seconded by Dr. Schmidt.

WHEREAS, It has become apparent that this Committee and the present Secretary and Librarian of the Chicago Historical Society, Mr. Charles Evans, cannot longer work together harmoniously, and that concord between the Committee and the Secretary and Librarian of the Society is necessary to the attainment of the purposes for which the Society was organized; and

WHEREAS, It is considered that good cause exists for terminating the relations aforesaid existing between said Evans and said Society, therefore be it, and it is hereby,

Resolved, That the said Charles Evans be, and he is hereby, discharged and removed from the said position of Secretary and Librarian of the Chicago Historical Society; and he is hereby requested and directed immediately to turn over and deliver to the President of said Society, who is now appointed and authorized to receive the same, all the keys to the doors of said Society's building, No. 142 Dearborn Avenue, in the City of Chicago, and to surrender to the said President all such possession or right of possession of said building, and of all property of said Society, as he, the said Evans, may heretofore have had as such Secretary and Librarian; and be it, and it is hereby, further

Resolved, That the Trustees of the Gilpin Fund, by whom the salary of the said Secretary and Librarian has heretofore been paid, be, and they are hereby, requested to pay to said Charles Evans any balance of salary, at the rate of eighteen hundred dollars ($1800) per year, which may be due him, or which would become due to him if he had continued to be such Secretary and Librarian, up to the first day of December, A. D. 1901. Unanimously adopted. . . . .

Moved by Dr. Schmidt that Miss Caroline M. McIlvaine be appointed Librarian of the Society until further notice of the Executive Committee at a monthly salary of $75.00. Carried.

The Executive Committee proceeds, on December 3, 1901, to inaugurate a new regime by stipulating the duties and fixing the salaries of the Society's employees.

The following resolutions were offered by Mr. Ayer, seconded by Mr. Merryweather and adopted by the Executive Committee:

Resolved, That the employees of the Chicago Historical Society shall, for the present consist of the following:

A Secretary, whose duties shall be to have charge, under the direction of the Executive Committee, of the building, books and everything pertaining to the Chicago Historical Society's collection. He shall be responsible for everything pertaining to same.

He shall conduct all correspondence.

A Librarian, whose duties shall be to classify and catalogue the library, under the direction of the Secretary and to do such other work as the Secretary may direct, and, in his absence, to take charge of the building, books and everything pertaining to same.

The salary of the Librarian shall for the present be not to exceed $75.00 per month.

A stenographer, whose duties shall be to assist the Librarian in classifying and cataloguing the library and to do such other work as directed by the Secretary and Librarian.

The salary of the Stenographer shall for the present be not to exceed $50.00 per month.

A Clerk, whose duties shall be to work under the direction of the Secretary and Librarian in connection with anything that is to be done in the library and building.

The salary of the Clerk shall for the present be not to exceed $35.00 per month.

A Messenger, whose duties shall be to work under the direction of the Secretary and Librarian and who will be expected to do anything he may be called on to do.

The salary of the Messenger shall, for the present, be not to exceed $20.00 per month.

A Janitor, whose duties shall be to keep the library and building clean, under the direction of the Secretary and Librarian and to do such other work as he may be called upon to perform.

The salary of the Janitor shall, for the present, be not to exceed $55.00 per month.

All of the above mentioned employees shall be engaged by the month and the services of any or all may be dispensed with at any time upon thirty days' notice on either side.

《 *Fernando Jones, one of the oldest residents of Chicago and long an honored member of the Society, entertains the members at a special meeting on March 17, 1903.*

At 8 o'clock P.M. on the above date a special meeting of the Society was held in the Lecture Hall of the Society's building, pursuant to notice duly given. President Jewett presided and introduced the speaker of the evening.

The speaker of the evening was Mr. Fernando Jones, a resident of Chicago since 1833, who addressed the Society and its guests on the subject: "The Indians of the Vicinity of Chicago and Anecdotes of Early Settlers." Mr. Jones wore an Indian costume, presented to him by his Indian admirers more than sixty years ago.

The audience numbered more than four hundred persons, being the largest number present at any meeting of the Society since the opening of the new building in November, 1896. The audience was highly entertained, and duly appreciated the instruction and information.

Fernando Jones was, among other things, a poetaster. His papers in the Chicago Historical Society contain a sheaf of verses in manuscript, among them the following.

<blockquote>
We left the parlor early
   I think 'twas scarcely nine
And by a happy fortune
   Her room was next to mine.
Resolved like old Columbus
   New regions to explore,
I took a snug position
   By the key-hole in the door.

The maiden then disrobing
   Revealed her pretty breasts;
Two round snowy hillocks,
   All crimsoned at the crest;
</blockquote>

And as she gently stroked them
   I softly cried, "Encore,"
But oh! she could not hear me
   Through the key-hole in the door.

She next unloosed her tresses,
   Of wavy chestnut hair,
Which fell in streaming torrents
   Adown her shoulders fair.
Then quickly she rebound them
   More firmly than before:
I watched the pretty process
   Through the key-hole in the door.

Then down upon the carpet
   She sat with graceful ease,
And raised her spotless linen,
   Above her snowy knees.
A dainty sky-blue garter
   On either leg she wore,
Oh! 'twas a glowing picture
   Through the key-hole in the door.

Now she the fire approaches,
   Her little feet to warm,
And nothing but a chemise
   Concealed her lovely form.
Thinks I, take off your chemise,
   I'll ask for nothing more,
And faith, I saw her do it,
   Through the key-hole in the door.

And next with nimble fingers
   She dons her snow-white gown
And on her bed fair Jennie
   Prepared to lay her down.
Upon a downy pillow
   She gently lays her head,
The light was then extinguished
   And darkness veiled the bed.

Ye dreaming men of science
   Who strain your eager eyes
In gazing at the planets
   That deck the distant skies,
Nature has greater wonders
   Than are dreamed of in your lore,
And a telescope is nothing
   To a key-hole in the door.

❲ *In the hundred years of its existence the Chicago Historical Society has received many bequests, but no other like that of Ossian Guthrie. The bequest is recorded in the* Tribune *of June 24, 1906.*

"I, Ossian Guthrie, being of sound mind and memory, do hereby give and bequeath to Samuel H. Kerfoot Jr., to be held in trust for the City of Chicago, all my knowledge of the earlier history of said City of Chicago pertaining to the arrival of Father Marquette, his residence here and his departure therefrom, said knowledge to be preserved and handed down to posterity. Ossian Guthrie."

Chicago has received from one of its pioneer residents

perhaps the oddest bequest ever made. Ossian Guthrie has bequeathed to Chicago and the world through S. H. Kerfoot Jr. and the Chicago Historical Society, all his knowledge of the first settlement of the city and of the surrounding country and secured for posterity the history of Marquette's arrival at Chicago. . . . . Instead of writing the history, Mr. Guthrie hit upon the plan of showing to the Historical Society, represented by Mr. Kerfoot, the spots and telling the stories.

He declares he expects to live twenty-five years, but would not take any chances of dying without leaving the world a record of Marquette's historic camps, churches and cabins that he has gained in fifty years of investigation.

He insisted on making the bequest personally so as to be sure it was correct, and the *Chicago Historical Society arranged an expedition to accompany him to record the stories and to photograph and mark the historic spots.*

The expedition, consisting of Miss Caroline M. McIlvaine, librarian of the Historical Society, Samuel H. Kerfoot Jr., Dr. Otto L. Schmidt, with T. A. O'Shaughnessy, the artist, as official photographer, went over the route traversed by Father Marquette 233 years ago.

Arrangements were made that Mr. O'Shaughnessy should make the photographs and arrange with local artists to paint pictures of the historic spots pointed out by Mr. Guthrie as they conceive them to have been when Father Marquette arrived and as they are today.

Mr. Guthrie started his bequest by giving to Mr. Kerfoot and his companions a view of the site of Marquette's winter camp of 1674 and 1675, where the adventurous pioneer erected the first cabin ever built in what is now Chicago.

This cabin stood upon a mound of silt at a point where

now Robey Street runs down to the west branch of the Chicago River. On the top of this mound Father Marquette pitched his tents in the winter of 1674. The site of the mound was on the north bank of the river, a few yards east of the spot where the drainage channel connects with the river.

At the time Father Marquette camped there the mound was 150 feet wide, nearly 350 feet long and approximately 16 feet high, and it was covered with a thick growth of scrub oak and other trees and with underbrush. It was composed of alluvial silt and it had been thrown up by a small stream that at that time flowed into the river from the south, just west of the mound.

Today there remains no sign of the mound and nothing to show where it stood, except the remains of the glacial drift under the surface.

Marquette's mound was used in rebuilding Chicago after the great fire of 1871. It was used to dust the molds in which the brick were made. For years the historical sand went to aid in the rebuilding of the city, and in 1880 the last of the mound disappeared and now the site is covered with the tall piles of lumber of great lumber yards.

Mr. Guthrie located the site of Marquette's cabin in 1847, when he was in charge of the Bridgeport pumping station, but not until he had spent fifty years of careful research did he give out the story as authentic, and the party that accompanied him, was the first to visit the spot with a full knowledge of its historic importance.

The next spot visited by the party was "The Summit," which lies to the south of Riverside on the south bank of the old tadpole ditch—the Illinois and Michigan Canal. A monument marks the spot and the bronze tablet tells the story:

Father Marquette
Landed Here in 1675

On March 31, 1675, Father Marquette was flooded out from his winter quarters on the silt mound at the foot of Robey Street, and the following day he went in a canoe and landed at "The Summit." The spot was located by a comparison of Marquette's journal with the original surveys of the county and made certain by the fact that "The Summit" is one of the striking landmarks of the country and minutely described by Marquette.

The monument at "The Summit" is constructed of boulders brought from the Lake Superior region by glaciers, and the glaciers that bore the boulders to the region hewed out the trail over which Marquette later traveled.

The monument was erected by the Chicago and Alton railway August 1895 to mark the spot.

After "The Summit" had been visited and photographed Mr. Guthrie gave the trustees of his legacy a taste of what Father Marquette endured. Leading them about 400 yards from the monument, he took them into the portage where Marquette and his party in August 1673 carried his canoes from the Desplaines River into the old channel which led into Mud Lake and from Mud Lake into the Chicago River.

Since Marquette's time the Illinois and Michigan Canal and the Drainage Canal have been cut through between "The Summit" and the portage, but the river at this point practically is unchanged and retains much of the primitive beauty that caused Father Marquette to name it "The Divine River." The portage practically is as it was when the priest-explorer hauled his birch bark canoes over it.

Over this portage Mr. Guthrie led the party, showing

them the spots of interest, following the route marked by Marquette and afterwards used by other pioneers, until they arrived at Prescott's Island, at the east end of the portage.

During the last part of the bequest the party advanced in a heavy thunder storm, and when they saw the spot where Father Marquette launched his canoes, Mr. Guthrie orally signed his bequest and turned over his historic knowledge to Mr. Kerfoot in trust for Chicago.

❲ *The Society makes a gala occasion of the fiftieth anniversary of its incorporation—February 7, 1907. The record of the proceedings quoted here is taken from a special publication,* Chicago Historical Society, 1857–1907, *issued soon after the celebration.*

The fiftieth anniversary of the incorporation of the Chicago Historical Society was marked by a special meeting of the Society and a reception in its building, on the evening of Thursday, February 7, 1907. Some two thousand invitations had been sent to its members, friends, and correspondents and more than four hundred persons were present at the exercises. . . . .

When the hour arrived for the exercises of the occasion, the audience assembled in the Lecture Hall in such numbers as to exhaust its seating capacity and many gentlemen stood through the entire programme.

On the stage beside the President were Messrs. Ezra B. McCagg, Elijah Kent Hubbard, and Erwin Doak Mead. President Head stated to the audience that Mr. McCagg was the sole surviving Charter Member and Incorporator of the Chicago Historical Society; that Mr. Erwin D. Mead of

Boston was the Vice-President and a working member of the Massachusetts Historical Society; that Mr. Hubbard was one of the first white children born in Chicago. He also announced that the Executive Committee had some weeks since invited Governor Deneen to be present and deliver an address, appropriate to the occasion, and read a letter from the Governor expressing his regret that imperative official duties had at the last moment obliged him to remain in Springfield, and extending to the Society his congratulations on its semi-centennial anniversary and wishing it prosperity for the future. . . . .

President Head then introduced Mr. McCagg, who reminisced about the history of the Society. In the course of his remarks he spoke particularly of the first president and first secretary-librarian.

". . . . An organization was had [in April, 1856], William H. Brown being the first president, and William Barry recording secretary and librarian. Mr. Brown was an old resident of the State. He came to Illinois in December, 1818, the population of the State at that time was not over 40,000, settled in Kaskaskia, then the seat of government, choosing Illinois because it had that summer adopted a free government, and purchased a one-half interest in the 'Illinois Intelligencer,' which paper dated back to 1815, and was the first newspaper published in the Territory. In 1823, he was at that time living in Vandalia, he did valiant work with pen and voice on the side of the Free-State party when an effort was made looking toward and intending the adoption of a new constitution permitting slavery. His activity in this direction did not increase his popularity in that region and an incipient effort was made to mob his paper. In 1835, he removed to Chicago. These facts are not, perhaps, quite germane here, yet they give some description of the man. The contest he had made was as close and impassioned as it was momentous. Suppose that at the commencement of the Civil War, Illinois had been a slave-state, supporting the secession column, the whole machinery of the state government in the hands of the South! Knowing him well, I linger about his name, because of the early stand he took which but foreshadowed in its regard for the right every action of his life. . . . .

"The Rev. William Barry, a Unitarian clergyman in delicate health and because of it without a charge, [was] the very embodiment of a collector of historical matter. No pamphlet so small or so apparently valueless but it was worth preserving if it but contained, not what was then, but what would sometime be worth something, historically. No elderly man who knew personally some historical incident but he would have him commit it to paper or, if he would, to write the history of his times, and many apparently ephemeral publications proved sometimes valuable almost immediately. He once, not many years later, asked the Galena and Chicago Railroad Company, or its successor, for a bound set of its reports. It had already become a leaf in the history of western progress. The answer came, that with great regret the road had to admit that it had not a full set; two years or more, as I recollect, were lacking. He was able to supply them. He had cared for them, year by year, as they appeared. He did most of the active work for years, the earlier ones, gratuitously, later, but after some years, for a small, very small compensation till want of strength required him to stop. Writing to Mr. Mason, president of the Society, a few years ago in response to a request from him for some information about Mr. Barry, I replied, and I can but repeat it here, 'He attended to the correspondence, unpacked the boxes, was most earnest and untiring in soliciting exchanges, made up the packages to be sent in return, kept the records including the minutes of meetings, went day by day in summer and in winter, in sunshine and in storm to the post-office for the mail, and carried in his arms, or even if very bulky on his back, heavy bundles of papers and books to the Society rooms. . . . .' "

Following Mr. McCagg, President Head related some of his own experiences as a member and officer of the Society.

"I am not an early member of the Historical Society, having joined in 1890, and my reminiscences are mostly measured by the terms in office of Mr. Edward G. Mason and Mr. John N. Jewett. I had occasionally, at an earlier date, attended the public meetings of the Society during the presidency of Mr. E. B. Washburne, the predecessor of Mr. Mason. His life-work illustrates anew the fact that America is the land of opportunity. Mr. Washburne, whose home, for the greater part of his life, was at Galena, was for many years a member of Congress; later, Secretary of State in the cabinet of President Grant; then Minister to France. Returning to America, and taking up his abode in Chicago, he sprang almost at once from the comparatively obscure position of French Ambassador to the presidency of the Chicago Historical Society, which position he held until his death. He was a most affable and dignified presiding officer, much interested in the work of the Society, and contributed to its shelves many volumes and public documents of value. His work here was a fitting crown of a laborious and honorable life.

"Mr. Edward G. Mason, after serving for several years

as the efficient Vice-President of the Society, was chosen as its President in 1887, and was annually re-elected for eleven years thereafter. His special work was the erection of the building which shelters us tonight. This building cost $190,-000. Nearly one-half this cost was borne by the donation of Henry D. Gilpin. The next largest item was $25,000 from John Crerar. After this were perhaps twenty others, subscribing amounts from $250 to $6000, such subscriptions being secured almost wholly by the efforts of Mr. Mason. The amount finally raised was said by the architect, Henry Ives Cobb, to be sufficient to complete the building, but when it was finished there was a deficiency of about $20,000. This was ultimately paid, one half by the gift of Mr. George M. Pullman, and the other half by the generous bequest of Mrs. J. Y. Scammon. The Society thus now owns the building and contents, free from debt. The building is the permanent monument to Mr. Mason. He was its inspiring genius.

"Mr. Mason was, in many ways, an ideal citizen of Chicago, the city of his pride and love. She never had a more loyal son. The growth of the city in material wealth, and especially in the cultivation and development of the arts, which are made possible by accumulated capital, was to him, a source of constant joy; and to the development of those arts, few contributed more than he.

"For the purpose of securing manuscripts and other material concerning the early history of Illinois, which were in danger of being lost, Mr. Mason spent many months, visiting all parts of Illinois and the neighboring states, and portions of Canada. Wherever he was, and however engaged, he always had an eye alert for adding anything of value to the splendid collection which now enriches this building. This collection is without parallel in the Nation, when we consider the brief time and limited means available for the work. . . . .

"Hon. John N. Jewett was chosen President of the Society in 1899, a year after the death of Mr. Mason, and filled the position until his death in 1904. Mr. Jewett had been for many years one of the leading members of the Chicago bar, and a diligent student of American history, especially the history of the region now known as the Middle West. He was thus fitted for the work to which he was called, and performed the duties of the position with conscientious fidelity. He almost never missed a meeting of the Society or its officers, and his sound judgment was of constant value in the management of its affairs. . . . .

"The records of the Society make mention of many interesting incidents during the past fifty years. In 1880, the Society was troubled by the existence of a mortgage of $12,000 upon its then new building, the holders of which were pressing for payment. At a meeting of the Executive Committee, where this matter had been discussed, Mr. L. Z. Leiter asked that he might be allowed to attend to that. A little memorandum book is now in the possession of the Society, showing the results of Mr. Leiter's activity as a canvasser. It shows that Judge Mark Skinner, Edwin H. Sheldon, Henry J. Willing, and Mr. Leiter himself, each contributed $2500, and Dr. D. K. Pearsons and Albert A. Munger each $1000, whereby the mortgage was cancelled. Mr. Leiter was for many years a liberal giver for the work of the Society. He paid the expense of publishing the first and second volumes of its collections.

"The unique and valuable papers of President James Madison, filling eight large folio volumes, which contain some fourteen hundred letters written by Mr. Madison, with some few received by him, during his public life, were purchased by Mr. Marshall Field, and presented by him to the Society. He also paid the cost of publishing the third volume of its collections, being the official letters and documents of Ninian Edwards, territorial governor of Illinois. . . . .

"The list of men and women who have been officers and members of the Historical Society is a notable one, and embraces a goodly proportion of the men who are credited with being the makers of Chicago. Among them we find the names of William B. Ogden, Isaac N. Arnold, Henry D. Gilpin, J. Y. Scammon, Walter L. Newberry, Edwin H. Sheldon, Cyrus H. McCormick, Henry J. Willing, T. B. Blackstone, N. K. Fairbank, George M. Pullman, Levi Z. Leiter, Mark Skinner, Marshall Field, William Blair, Charles B. Farwell, S. H. Kerfoot, Dr. R. N. Isham, Edwin C. Larned, Henry W. King, Edwin S. Isham, Wm. G. Hibbard, C. W. Fullerton, John H. Dunham, George Sturges, Chalkley J. Hambleton, Julian S. Rumsey, John B. Turner, Jonathan Burr, Dr. John H. Foster, William Bross, A. H. Burley, Hugh T. Dickey, H. G. Loomis, J. H. McVicker, F. H. Winston, John Wentworth, J. T. Ryerson, Thomas Hoyne, Ezra B. McCagg, Lambert Tree, D. K. Pearsons, Henry H. Porter, A. C. Bartlett, E. W. Blatchford, Byron L. Smith, Edward E. Ayer, Samuel M. Nickerson, Richard T. Crane, D. G. Hamilton, Charles L. Hutchinson, Martin A. Ryerson, John J. Glessner, Ezra J. Warner, and many more of the builders of our city. We feel therefore, when we invite the men and women of the present and the coming generation to join this notable band of honorable men and women, that we are asking them to marry into a good and worthy family.

"The meeting of this evening is designed to be largely social, where the old and the newer members of the Society may meet and become acquainted. Nothing in the way of passing the plate is contemplated. But it may not be amiss to briefly advert to the financial side of the work of the Society. I have already stated that the institution owns its building and collections, and is free from debt. Its income is derived from the annual dues of the members, and the interest upon its permanent endowment. This endowment is regretfully small. It is carefully invested, but the income is greatly inadequate to the work before its managers. Rare and valuable material connected with the early history of our city and State, that will be of priceless value to the future historian and which may at any time, be lost or destroyed, is often available, but we have not the money to buy when it is purchasable.

"Within the last few years, several sums of $5000 and some of lesser amounts, have been bequeathed for the endowment fund, by Mrs. Edward Swan Stickney, Mrs. J. Y. Scammon, Mrs. Mahlon D. Ogden, Mrs. Lucian Tilton, Huntington W. Jackson, Henry J. Willing, E. T. Watkins, and T. Mauro Garrett.

"I trust that these items indicate a growing habit among the members of the Society to remember it in their wills, and few methods can be named where the memory of the donors, attached to a special fund, will be more sure of permanent honor, or where the donations will be used more for the benefit of Chicago and its people, and its men and women of letters. . . . ."

Following the applause with which President Head's address was received, the audience left the Lecture Hall and found entertainment in the various departments of the building. The Gilpin Library, the Stickney Library, the Manuscript Room, and the Museum, all were open and each attracted its quota of the guests. Refreshments were served on the large bronze tables in the Reading Room, where the decorations were American Beauty roses, and a special exhibit of photographs, manuscripts, and other monuments of the first days of the Society, arranged by the House Committee and the Librarian, bore eloquent testimony to the foresight of the founders. A large number of ladies and gentlemen present had been residents of Chicago for the whole fifty years of the Society's life, and this gathering gave to these people such an opportunity as had rarely been offered of meeting a goodly number of their friends and acquaintances of early days.

⟨ *On December 8, 1908, the Society holds a Roosevelt meeting—accepting a portrait of the President and electing him to Honorary Membership.*

On Tuesday evening, December 8, the Society tendered a reception to its members and invited guests upon the occasion of the presentation by Mr. Henry C. Lytton of a life-size oil portrait of Theodore Roosevelt by August Benziger of Switzerland. Mr. Head occupied the chair and Mr. Lytton, Mr. August Benziger, the artist, and Dr. Frank W. Gunsaulus, who made the presentation address, had seats upon the platform.

The name of Theodore Roosevelt previously recommended by the Executive Committee for election by the Society to Honorary Membership, was presented and he was unanimously elected. A characteristically cordial letter from President Roosevelt was read before the meeting.

THE WHITE HOUSE
Washington

December 4, 1908

MY DEAR MR. HEAD:

Indeed it will give me great pleasure to accept honorary membership in the Chicago Historical Society. I know its work well, and in the past have again and again been thrown into intimate associations with various men among its members. I assure you I appreciate the compliment paid me.

With regards, I am,
Sincerely yours,
THEODORE ROOSEVELT

Mr. Franklin H. Head,
President, Chicago Historical Society
Dearborn Avenue and Ontario Street,
Chicago

In accepting Honorary Membership in the Chicago Historical Society, President Roosevelt joined a distinguished company. In the half-century of its existence the Society had conferred this honor on sixty-two men and two women. Their names follow.

CHARLES FRANCIS ADAMS	JOHN BRIGHT
SAMUEL GREENE ARNOLD	LEWIS CASS
GEORGE BANCROFT	RICHARD COBDEN
WILLIAM H. BISSELL	EDWARD COLES
HENRY WILLIAMS BLODGETT	SHELBY M. CULLOM
MASON BRAYMAN	STEPHEN A. DOUGLAS
SIDNEY BREESE	ANDREW SLOAN DRAPER

THOMAS DRUMMOND
EDWARD EVERETT
MICHEL ETIENNE FAILLON
GEORGE BARTHOLOMEW
    FARIBAULT
THOMAS FOLEY
LADY JANE GRIFFIN
    FRANKLIN
FRANCOIS XAVIER GARNEAU
JOSEPH EASTON GARY
DESIRE GIROUARD
OSSIAN GUTHRIE
SAMUEL SMITH HARRIS
GEORGE FREDERICK
    WILLIAM HOLLS
GURDON SALTONSTALL
    HUBBARD
EDMUND JANES JAMES
JOHN FRANKLIN JAMESON
FERNANDO JONES
DAVID KING
JULIETTE A. MAGILL
    KINZIE
JOHANN GEORG KOHL
ABRAHAM LINCOLN
WILLIAM EDWARD
    McLAREN
JOHN McMULLEN
PIERRE MARGRY
MATTHEW FONTAINE
    MAURY

CHARLES DELEVAN MOSHER
JOHN LOTHROP MOTLEY
HENRY PELHAM CLINTON,
    DUKE OF NEWCASTLE
FREDERICK NOLTE
RICHARD J. OGLESBY
PETER PARKER
WILLIAM FREDERICK POOLE
HORATIO NELSON POWERS
WILLIAM HICKLING
    PRESCOTT
JOHN REYNOLDS
CHARLES ROGERS
JAMES SAVAGE
HENRY SHAW
GOLDWIN SMITH
JARED SPARKS
ADLAI EWING STEVENSON
WILLIAM LEETE STONE, JR.
CHARLES SUMNER
LYMAN TRUMBULL
JAMES BARR WALKER
SAMUEL DEXTER WARD
FREDERIC COPE
    WHITEHOUSE
ROBERT CHARLES
    WINTHROP
RICHARD YATES
SIR JOHN YOUNG,
    BARON LISGAR

❧ *With all the rest of the United States the Society celebrates the one hundredth anniversary of Lincoln's birth. The first of a series of meetings is described in the minutes of the Executive Committee.*

On Friday evening, January 15, 1909, at a special meeting held in the Lecture Hall, the Society inaugurated its celebration of the Centenary of the birth of Abraham Lincoln when William Webster Ellsworth, Secretary of the Century Company, New York City, delivered an illustrated lecture entitled, "Abraham Lincoln, Boy and Man."

. . . . Mr. Ellsworth gave to his audience the fruit of many years of thought and research both in anecdote and illustration. In the latter, he was particularly fortunate in being able to show to his audience many unique treasures from such collections of Lincolniana as Major Lambert's, of Philadelphia, and by permission of the publishers of Nicolay and Hay's and Miss Tarbell's biographies of Lincoln some of their original illustrations were used.

The result was a wonderful wealth of material regarding Lincoln, especially concerning his early years in Illinois. The meeting attracted a large audience, many of whom remembered with pleasure Mr. Ellsworth's lecture before the Society some years ago: "From Lexington to Yorktown."

CHICAGO HISTORICAL SOCIETY

DEARBORN AVENUE AND ONTARIO STREET.

The Chicago Historical Society invites you to attend a special meeting of the Society, at which William Webster Ellsworth, of New York City, will deliver an illustrated lecture, entitled,

"ABRAHAM LINCOLN: BOY AND MAN,"

Friday evening, Jan. 15, 1909, at eight o'clock

The climactic meeting comes, as it should, on February 12. Again the minutes of the Executive Committee furnish the record. (The minutes, however, convey no idea of Colonel Carr's truly remarkable histrionic feat, the Colonel being a man of ordinary height, but of such huge girth that he appeared to be almost round.)

On the evening of February 12 at 8 o'clock the Society held a special meeting in commemoration of the One Hundredth Anniversary of the birth of Abraham Lincoln, which was attended by an audience that taxed the capacity of the Lecture Hall, many being turned away for lack of room. . . . .

President Head introduced the speaker of the evening, Colonel Clark E. Carr, of Galesburg, Illinois, whose subject was "Lincoln at Gettysburg." Col. Carr was present at the dedication of the Gettysburg National Cemetery as delegate from Illinois, and occupied a seat on the platform not far from Lincoln when he uttered those immortal words. During the course of his address he recited the Gettysburg Speech as he remembered it spoken by President Lincoln, imitating his voice and manner, which is said by those who knew Lincoln to be quite remarkable in its faithfulness to the original. . . . .

Miss McIlvaine, evaluating the Lincoln Centenary, sees in the interest it aroused an earnest of what the Society, with greater facilities, might accomplish.

The week of February 8 to 13 will be a memorable one in the annals of the Society for many reasons, but more particularly because of the unprecedented number of children

who visited the exhibition of Lincolniana. . . . . More than
a thousand viewed the exhibit during Lincoln week.

The greater number of the children came in classes accompanied by the principals or teachers of the schools, and
with few exceptions the latter expressed to the librarian and
assistants their appreciation of the high educational value of
the exhibit. The children of course carried the news of the
collections displayed here into hundreds of homes where
this work had never been heard of before and the result can
not fail to be a wider field of influence for the Society. The
Society's guests numbered 500 on the evening of February
12th giving a total attendance for the week of 1500.

Among the visitors who signed the register on February
18th was Ambassador Bryce who, accompanied by Mr. Robert
T. Lincoln, spent nearly an hour in the building. . . . .

Visitors to the Lincoln exhibit continued to the end of
the month, and many expressed regret that the collection
could not be permanently on exhibition. Now that the time
has arrived when the various interesting portraits must be
taken down and replaced in their wrappings to be stored
away because there is no wall space available to display them,
the thought comes that by so doing not only the public but the
Society is suffering a distinct loss in that it is deprived of a
channel of educational and inspirational influence which it
would seem desirable to keep open. If there were a room
even of moderate size where could be grouped the manuscripts, portraits and relics now owned by the Society to be
known as the "Abraham Lincoln Room" there is no question
that additions of value would be contributed and in time this
might become a fitting and permanent memorial that Chicago
people would be proud of.

❡ *The Lincoln celebration ushered in a succession of cen-*
tennial observances in each of which the Society would take
a leading part. Next came the one hundredth anniversary of
the Fort Dearborn Massacre. Miss McIlvaine is the reporter.

At eight o'clock on the evening of Thursday, August 15,
1912, the Chicago Historical Society, the United States
Daughters of 1812 and the Society of the War of 1812 assembled in joint session in the Historical Society's building,
to commemorate the One Hundredth Anniversary of the
Fort Dearborn Massacre which occurred August 15, 1812.
Colonel Nathan William MacChesney, President of the Society of the War of 1812, was the orator of the evening.
President Dent presided and by his invitation there were on
the stage the following guests of honor:—

Colonel Nathan William MacChesney, President of the
Society of the War of 1812,

Mrs. Samuel W. Early, President of the United States
Daughters of 1812,

Mrs. Martha Heald Johnson, of New York, grand-
daughter of Captain Nathan Heald, the commander of Fort
Dearborn at the time of the Massacre,

Mrs. Eva Spaulding Corthell, of Jacksonville, Fla., the
great granddaughter of Captain William Wells,

Mr. James Whistler Wood, grandson of Captain John
Whistler, the builder of Fort Dearborn,

Miss Josephine Jarvis, of Cobden, Illinois, daughter of
Joseph Russell Jarvis, a midshipman on the *Constitution* in
1812, and

Mrs. Martha Haskell Ten Eyck whose father was a soldier in the War of 1812.

The exercises were opened by Judge Dent who, in a few graceful words, announced the purpose of the joint meeting, and proceeded at once to make the formal presentation of a painting of Fort Dearborn in 1857 by the late Dwight Benton, on behalf of the widow and sister of the artist, Mrs. Dwight Benton, of Rome, Italy, and Mrs. Delia Benton Legg, of Coldwater, Michigan.

Judge Dent then introduced Mrs. Early who read a brief account of the United States Daughters of 1812, and told of the excellent work they have done in locating and marking the graves of Illinois soldiers in the War of 1812.

In a few brief sentences the President alluded to the event that was commemorated in this meeting and introduced Colonel MacChesney. The address which followed was one that will doubtless linger in the memories of those who heard it as the clearest and most eloquent exposition of the causes of the Second War with Great Britain and of the part played in it by the garrison of Fort Dearborn, that it has been their privilege to hear.

It may be doubted if the hundreds who followed with intentness, as the speaker pictured the sequence of events in the Fort and on the lake shore on that morning one hundred years ago, can hereafter pass along the streets and boulevards that have taken the place of the lake shore trail without reverting in memory to those acts of heroism that make this ground sacred.

There was great applause at the close of the address, and on motion of Mr. Henry E. Hamilton, seconded by Mr. Gunther, the thanks of the Society were extended to Colonel MacChesney.

Thus closed the formal program, all of which was stenographically reported and on invitation of the President the audience moved to the main hall where light refreshments were served and an informal reception in honor of the descendants of the participants of the Massacre was held until a late hour. On taking their departure many expressed themselves amply gratified in having a part in the Society's observance of the centennial anniversary.

There were 350 members and guests present.

❨ *The Douglas Centenary follows in less than a year. Judging from Miss McIlvaine's report, Colonel Carr portrays Douglas as effectively as he had impersonated Lincoln.*

More than a year ago the Chairman of the Entertainment Committee expressed the hope that the Society might be able to fittingly commemorate the One Hundredth Anniversary of the birth of Stephen Arnold Douglas, April 23, 1913. It is altogether probable that had it not been for this forethought, the centenary of Chicago's most widely known citizen would have passed unmarked, for although he was a generous benefactor of the city as well as a great statesman, the fame of Stephen A. Douglas seems to have become strangely obscured. . . . .

Mr. Martin F. Douglas, grandson of Stephen A. Douglas, having arrived the evening before to represent his father in the commemoration, was escorted to the [Douglas] Monument by eighteen members of the Historical Society, the party going to the Monument by automobiles. Notable among these were, Col. Francis A. Eastman, Wm. J. Onahan, Horatio L. Wait and Redmond Prindiville, all of whom were members of the Douglas Funeral Committee in 1861; Henry

E. Hamilton, who was one of the organizers of the Douglas Invincibles; Henry Greenbaum, who made speeches for Douglas throughout Illinois in 1860; others were Bishop Cheney, Elias Colbert, Frederick A. Barnard, W. D. Kerfoot, F. G. Logan, W. F. Dummer, Wm. H. Bush, and Julius Frankel. Messrs. Burley, Schmidt, Merryweather and Fuller represented the Executive Committee.

Mr. Burley introduced the speakers who were William J. Onahan, William Dillon, representing the Mayor, and Bishop Cheney. At the close of the exercises, a large vase of American Beauty roses tied with ribbons bearing the legend, "Stephen A. Douglas, 1813-1913. Chicago Historical Society," was placed within the tomb, which had been opened for the occasion, Dr. Schmidt having secured the permission of the South Park Commissioners to do this. . . . .

In the evening an audience that filled the Lecture Hall greeted Colonel Clark E. Carr, the orator of the occasion, and young Mr. Douglas who read a letter to the Society from his father, Hon. Robert M. Douglas, of Greensboro, N. C. It may be doubted if there is living today anyone who could have presented the facts of Douglas' career with greater fidelity than did Colonel Carr and it is very certain that nowhere could have been gathered hearers better able to judge of the faithfulness of the presentation, for again the audience contained many men and women who participated in the excitements of the "Joint Debates." Young Mr. Douglas made an excellent impression and it was said that his delivery recalled some of the characteristics of his grandfather. Mr. Wallace Rice, the son of John A. Rice, an early Chicago resident and an ardent advocate of the views of the "Little Giant," read an original ode entitled "Stephen A. Douglas."

With the impressive reading of the poem the memorable evening closed, but the guests lingered for an hour renewing friendships and examining the portraits and mementoes of Douglas exhibited in the south room.

(*The biggest celebration of all came in 1918, when Illinois observed the centennial of its admission to the Union. The fact that the nation was deep in the First World War put no damper on enthusiasm. The Society held its observance on April 19. Anticipating, rightly, a huge attendance, it moved to Orchestra Hall for the occasion.*

The Tribune *catches the spirit of a notable gathering.*

From far and near they came, in silks and satins and in threadbare serges, some young, but most of them old, to attend the centennial celebration of the statehood of Illinois by the Chicago Historical Society in Orchestra Hall last night. For an hour before the doors were opened they came, old ladies, with snowy white hair and faltering footsteps, leaning on the arms of their grandchildren, but interestedly talking of old times and greeting with enthusiasm other "old settlers."

There were old soldiers, often bent with rheumatism, but with pride in their eyes, for were they not partly responsible for Illinois' fame and glory? Every one who was in any way interested in the history of our state was there to help make the celebration the success that it was.

In the foyer was an exhibit of historical relics of unusual interest. Regimentals, firearms, and manuscripts of Revolutionary and Civil War days were side by side with quaint old bonnets and fans and other feminine trinkets that our great-grandmothers owned. One of the most interesting

Historia Rediviva   Chicago Salutatrix

1818—1918

THE CENTENNIAL OF ILLINOIS STATEHOOD
COMMEMORATED BY THE
CHICAGO HISTORICAL SOCIETY
IN ORCHESTRA HALL
ON THE EVENING OF APRIL NINETEENTH
MDCCCC XVIII

The Old Flags   The Old Songs
The Early Records   The Early Families

CENTENNIAL COMMITTEE

MR. CHARLES B. PIKE, Chairman   MRS. ROBT. HALL McCORMICK, JR
MRS. JOHN A. CARPENTER   MR. JULIAN S. MASON
MRS. KELLOGG FAIRBANK   MR. RALPH C. OTIS
MR. ROBERT C. FERGUS   MRS. BRONSON PECK
MRS. JAMES L. HOUGHTELING   MR. JOHN C. SHAFFER
MISS CAROLINE M. McILVAINE   MRS. FREDERICK T WEST

EX-OFFICIIS

MR. CLARENCE A. BURLEY, President, Chicago Historical Society
DR. OTTO L SCHMIDT, Vice-President, Chicago Historical Society, President of the Illinois
Centennial Commission

things was a pair of white kid gloves, yellowed with age, which were worn by Mrs. Thomas Mather (who was Hannah Lamb before her marriage) at a ball given for Lafayette in Kaskaskia on April 30, 1825. On each glove was reproduced a miniature of the Frenchman.

There were also relics of the Indian days—tomahawks and other weapons of massacre. On the walls were hung portraits of former governors of the state, and in the hall were paintings of Illinois. Before the program began a stringed orchestra in the hall played the old tunes, carrying many a person present back to the days of long ago when he or she sang those very songs.

On the stage, which was decorated with old flags, sat the members of the choruses, Clarence A. Burley, president of the Historical Society; Charles B. Pike, chairman of the centennial committee of the Society; the Rt. Rev. Charles P. Anderson; Gov. Lowden, and many representatives of prominent pioneer families. The meeting was opened with patriotic songs, led by the chorus of the Civic Music Association, men of the St. Peter's Episcopal choir, and the Choral Society of the Commonwealth Edison Company.

Mr. Pike then introduced Mr. Burley, who made a short speech and introduced Bishop Anderson, the speaker of the evening.

Bishop Anderson told in glowing terms the history of Illinois from 1818 to the present and eulogized the persons who have been prominent in making the history. He closed his address by saying that Illinois had given the best of her manhood to both the Civil and Mexican wars and that she was doing the same now.

Miss Mina Hager sang a group of ballads popular in

recruiting camps at the outbreak of the Civil War, and members of Hand's orchestra gave a program of early dance music which set many of the old people's feet to keeping time.

Two of the most picturesque figures were Mrs. Mary C. Brown Tyler and Miss Marette Twitty, who were dressed in old fashioned costumes. Mrs. Tyler wore a magenta rep gown, which she had made in the late sixties to wear to the wedding of Miss Skinner and Henry Willing, the parents of Mark Skinner Willing, who is now in France. Her white hair was partially covered with a white lace cap and on her hands she wore white kid gloves with ruffled lace around the wrists. Miss Twitty's dress of sky blue taffeta with velvet stripes was first worn by an ancestor of hers at a reception to Jenny Lind in 1850 in New York City. Both of these dear little old ladies were the center of attention last night.

In the audience were Mr. and Mrs. Julian Mason, Mrs. John Borden, Mrs. Charles B. Pike, Mrs. Lorenzo M. Johnston, Mrs. Ayres Boal, Mrs. Raymond Hardenberg, Mrs. George B. Massey, Mrs. Frank O. Lowden, Mrs. W. B. Currier of Boston, Mrs. George M. Pullman, Mr. and Mrs. Cyrus Hall McCormick, Mr. and Mrs. Edward Garraghan, Mrs. H. M. Wilmarth, Mr. and Mrs. Edward O. Brown, Mrs. Cyrus H. Adams, Mrs. Elisha Whitehead, the Misses Williams, Mr. and Mrs. Edward G. Shumway, Judge and Mrs. T. G. Windes, Mr. and Mrs. Otto C. Butz, Mrs. Clarence A. Burley, Mrs. Treat Campbell, Miss E. V. Rumsey, Mr. and Mrs. William Nelson Pelouze, Mrs. James W. Scott, Mrs. Frederick W. Gookin, Mrs. Horace Kennedy, Mrs. Bronson Peck, Mr. and Mrs. Richard L. Pennington, Miss Caroline McIlvaine, Mrs. Robert Hall McCormick, Jr., Mrs. Frederick T. West, and Mrs. Donald McPherson.

❨ *In the spring of 1920 the Society embarks on one of the boldest ventures in its history. For fifty years Charles F. Gunther, candy manufacturer, alderman, and trustee of the Chicago Historical Society, had been amassing an enormous collection of art treasures, rare books and prints, manuscripts, and historic objects. He had stopped at nothing, even bringing Libby Prison from Richmond to Chicago. The private museum he maintained in his place of business had become one of the sights of the city, attracting thousands of visitors annually. Gunther died on February 10, 1920. Six weeks later—on March 26—the* Daily News *reported that the Gunther collection would go to the Historical Society.*

The uncataloged, mysterious, and almost priceless C. F. Gunther collection of manuscripts, relics, historical souvenirs, letters and documents is going to the Chicago Historical Society for $150,000. . . . .

The Chicago Historical Society hasn't bought the collection yet. But from authoritative sources it was learned that the meeting of directors yesterday held by the Society practically assured the famous collection for the institution.

"There is no doubt that the money will be raised in time," said Miss Caroline McIlvaine, librarian of the Society. "We will be able to sell a small part of the total collection for $150,000 and thus safeguard the men and women who guarantee the sum to the Guther estate. Nobody knows what is in the collection. The $300,000 value is fixed upon only that part of it that has been seen and examined by experts. But the rest—heavens! There are things there that are virtually priceless. Aside from its aesthetic value the collection is in itself the greatest historical value for Chicagoans the country affords."

The collection, in a state of excellent preservation, lies carefully stacked on the fourth floor of the Gunther building. There are American prints dating from colonial days in which the entire panorama of American life is reviewed.

The educational value of these prints is equal to their financial value, according to experts. They reveal the life of the colonies, the Revolution, the slow march west of the American republic, the pioneer life in Ohio, Wisconsin, Illinois, the plainsmen, the early Pennsylvania settlers, on through the occupation of the Mississippi valley, the rangers of the southwest, the "forty-niners," the birth of the far western towns. In them American history is given vivid outline "and," said Miss McIlvaine, "there's nothing like this single collection of prints alone in the world."

. . . . There are letters from Lincoln to Grant, declared to be more valuable than any in the possession of the Society. . . . . George Washington's compass and tea and camp dishes, ... the table on which Gen. Grant wrote the terms of surrender of Gen. Lee, Gen. Lee's farewell to his troops, French documents deeding Louisiana to the United States—these and thousands of other odds and ends, ranging from antiquity through the detailed historical past of Chicago—fill the treasure trove in the Gunther building.

"We don't want anybody else to share in the purchase of the collection," explained Miss McIlvaine and President Clarence A. Burley. "Its acquisition by our Society will mean the establishment of the Society as a model for all similar societies in the country. The Americana in the collection is the greatest Americanization force that can be assembled merely as propaganda."

On March 30 the Society's Executive Committee takes final action.

Resolved, That it is highly desirable that this Society purchase at the price of One Hundred and Fifty Thousand Dollars ($150,000.00) the entire collection of the Charles F. Gunther Estate, except the portraits, the Trustees being advised that the collection is worth much more than that sum. . . . . The right of purchase must be exercised immediately or it will be lost.

And further resolved, That the Society appeal to its friends and the public, and all who are interested in retaining in Chicago a very valuable, historical and educational collection, for subscriptions for this purpose.

Women interested in obtaining the collection for the Society lose no time in forming an organization and going into action. The Daily News *for April 14 reports their first step in arousing interest.*

There was a new attraction at the C. F. Gunther estate rooms at 1013 South Wabash Avenue yesterday. For days the miniatures, the historical documents, the first editions, the curios, have waited mutely. Yesterday afternoon the charms of Lincoln's stage coach, Margaret Carter's little satin slippers of the season 1776, Benedict Arnold's pass, the original revenue stamps that caused the Revolution and an original London newspaper in which there is the account of a king and a prince of Wales rushing buckets to a fire were augmented by a really modern attraction—a cup of tea.

The tea party, which may in the future be dubbed by the Chicago Historical Society "the Chicago Tea Party," was designed to save for the youth of Chicago the Gunther collection, which is to be sold for $150,000, one-half of its value.

A mast lamp and a pilot wheel of Admiral Perry's flagship, the *Powhatan*, and the oldest American service flag, captured at Drummond Island by the Chippewa Indians in 1812, were among the things that attracted attention. Women of old Chicago families who declared they would help to gain the collection for the Historical Society are Mrs. C. H. McCormick, Mrs. Robert B. Gregory, Mrs. George Isham, Mrs. George B. Carpenter, Mrs. Arthur Farwell, Mrs. Frederick T. West, Miss Elizabeth Faulkner, and Mrs. Horace Martin.

To raise $150,000 turns out to be a formidable undertaking, made more than ordinarily difficult by the depression of 1921. After more than three years, and several extensions, the Gunther heirs decide that they can wait no longer. To bring the purchase to a conclusion, they offer a concession. President Burley calls a special meeting of the Executive Committee for September 21, 1923.

The President, announcing the final adjustment of the Gunther Collection purchase as the special object of consideration for this meeting, stated that Mrs. C. F. Gunther and Captain Burnell Gunther had given an option to close the deal at an advantageous figure by October 1st, and that in case of non-acceptance of this option by the Society there would be much loss to the Society, and that he had been notified that after the first of October the entire balance due must be paid before November 1st or the contract between the Society and Mrs. and Captain Gunther would be cancelled.

The President stated that the sum arranged for the purchase of the Collection between the Gunther Estate and the Society had been $150,000; that this had been reduced to $29,861.97; that now Mrs. and Captain Gunther agreed to accept as final payment for the sale of the Gunther Collection to the Society the sum of $25,400, of which $2,000 was to be allowed for the California gold nugget to be returned. The delivery of this nugget was an essential feature of the bargain. On the balance of $23,400 was to be allowed payments recently made, $2,083.80, leaving to complete the bargain $21,316.20; that there was on hand in the Gunther Fund over $1,000, leaving still to be raised about $20,000; that there is in various funds of the Society, which are unrestricted as to their application and which under rulings of the Executive Committee had been invested, $23,500 of bonds, which could be sold to realize the balance needed. It will be seen that by this transaction a reduction of over $6,000 of the final payment would be obtained for the benefit of the Society. The gold nugget had been valued at $5,000, but in spite of numerous attempts it could not be sold at even $4,000. After considerable discussion, the following resolution was offered and seconded:

"*Resolved*, That the offer of Mrs. and Captain Gunther to accept for the final sum of $29,861.97 still due from the Society the sum of $21,316.20 in cash and the gold nugget as complete and final payment, be accepted, and that the President be and he is hereby authorized to sell such securities held in free and unrestricted funds of the Society as may be needed for the completion of this transaction."

The President put the question. Messrs. Busch, Loesch, Schmidt and the President voted "aye." Mrs. Carpenter did not vote.

〖 *In the presence of visiting royalty Americans usually make themselves more or less ridiculous. When Queen Marie of Romania—hardly top drawer—visited Chicago on November 14, 1926, one gathers from the* Tribune's *report that even the officials of the Historical Society behaved in character. The queen had started out the day by laying a wreath at the foot of Saint-Gaudens' "Lincoln" in Lincoln Park.*

. . . . The procession of half a dozen cars containing bodyguard, municipal officials, the royal children and their mother moved down North Dearborn Street to the Historical Society's grim brownstone castle at the corner of Dearborn and Ontario streets.

After unseemly clamor at the door—where the trustees of the institution were perspiring freely—as to who should be admitted, the hysterical part of that program was cleared away by apologies and the historical part began.

The queen had quick comment and quicker questions about everything she saw. The bed on which Mr. Lincoln died commanded her intent gaze. While she stood silent at its foot and looked, Dr. Otto Schmidt, her cicerone, dispensed copious information. Over the headboard of the bed a laurel wreath was draped. An American flag served for counterpane.

From the bed the queen turned to the sofa that was once a part of the furnishings of the Lincoln homestead. She regarded it judicially—like a housewife—then sat upon it, saying, "It doesn't look as comfortable as it is. Very nice!"—and with that exclamation she made a bouncy little motion on the old sofa.

She asked eager questions about the replica of Gutzon

189

Borglum's colossal head of Lincoln, which looks down upon the main court from the second gallery, and she paused with a cry of admiration before Rembrandt Peale's stately portrait of Washington. The wax figurines representing seventy-two of your notable townswomen during a century and a quarter of Chicago's annals caught her fancy. That pictorial glimpse into our past was supplemented with presentation to her by the Society of a copy of the first edition (1856) of the sole classic in our local literature, Mrs. John H. Kinzie's "Waubun: The Early Day in the Northwest."

At departure the queen signed the visitors' book with a big, bold "Marie"—and only that—and the children followed with their names in smaller script.

A

LARGER

CONCEPT

1927 – 1932

⟨ IN November, 1927, Charles B. Pike is elected President of the Chicago Historical Society. His goal, from the beginning, is the erection of a new and beautiful building which would house a museum of American history far in advance of anything of its kind. In little more than six months after Mr. Pike's election the Trustees announce plans.

Plans for a new $1,000,000 museum for the Chicago Historical Society to be erected in Lincoln Park near North Avenue and Clark Street in time for Chicago's centennial celebration were announced yesterday by the trustees of the Society.

The structure will take the place of the present inadequate home of the Society at Dearborn and Ontario streets. A new building with additional facilities is needed in order to exhibit to the best advantage the great number of records and objects depicting the history of Chicago and the Northwest that have been collected by the Society since its founding in 1856.

The plans call for construction of a modern fireproof and artistic building of the Georgian colonial type. It will be of brick with white marble or limestone trimming. Its architecture will correspond with that of the present buildings in the park. The architects are Graham, Anderson, Probst & White. Interior plans call for an auditorium for public lectures and entertainments as well as a number of special classrooms for children.

The bill which authorized the Park Commissioners to allocate a site for the museum was passed by the state legislature last February and became effective July 1. The terms agreed upon by the Park Commissioners and the trustees of the Society make it conditional that the Society complete the building within a period of five years.

"While detailed plans for the financing of the building have not yet developed it is expected that by early fall preparations will be well under way," President Charles B. Pike of the Historical Society said yesterday. "This new building will permit the people of Chicago to join in supporting a project which is created for the sole purpose of maintaining the traditions of the city, state and union as well as promoting the ideals of patriotism, civic service and progressive education."

Plans mature. The Society opens its campaign for funds on the evening of October 25, 1929.

Framed in a colonial setting and located in one of the most magnificent sites in the city, what Gov. Louis L. Emmerson last night termed "the legend of Illinois" is to be popularized and perpetuated by the Chicago Historical Society.

Plans for a new $1,500,000 home for the organization and its exhibits were announced last night at a meeting at the present building, at which the state's chief executive was the principal speaker.

Commendation and congratulation on both site and setting were forthcoming from William D. Saltiel, city attorney, representing Mayor Thompson; Eugene S. Taylor of the Chicago Plan Commission; President Walter Dill Scott of Northwestern University; Rowland Haynes, secretary of the University of Chicago; the Rev. Robert J. Kelley, president of Loyola University, and others.

Facing the Saint-Gaudens statue of Lincoln in Lincoln Park, near the corner of North Avenue and Clark Street, the new museum will be 300 feet long and 175 feet wide, of red brick with white limestone or tile trimming, to harmonize with the style of the administration building at Center Street.

It will have two stories and a basement and has been designed for the most efficient placing of exhibits and to eliminate the element of fatigue as much as possible.

Visitors will enter from the Dearborn Street side, to find themselves in the main foyer, facing a colonial staircase that leads up to the second floor. The ground floor will contain a series of rooms arranged to take the visitor in chronological order through every stage in American history from the time of Columbus down to the present. . . . .

"The entire state of Illinois," Gov. Emmerson told members of the Society last night, "is indebted to the Chicago Historical Society for having collected and preserved so many of the relics of the state as well as the city. It was largely through the example of this Society that the Illinois State Historical Society was formed. I wish you many years of luck in carrying on the legend of Illinois.

"Writers today have taken to disrobing our national heroes and belittling their characters. The story of Washington and the cherry tree probably is a legend, but why do away with a story that interests childhood and helps men and women to strengthen their own characters? Let us not think of George Rogers Clark as a man who carried a whisky flask, but as a hero who tramped through mire to his knees to serve his country. Similarly with Lincoln."

Charles B. Pike, President of the Society, was host at a dinner at the Chicago Club preceding the meeting for Gov. Emmerson and the other distinguished guests.

❪ *Normally, an event like the Society's meeting of October 25 would have been featured by every Chicago newspaper. Instead, the story was buried in the back pages. For nothing was normal on October 25, 1929. On the day before, the stock market had crashed with a thud that would reverberate for years. Twenty-four hours before the Society's meeting great black headlines darkened the front pages of every paper in the country. The* Daily News *announced: "Stocks Dive and Rebound in Record—Pass 11 Million Share Mark in Frenzied Sales." The* Evening Post *was more succinct—and more ominous: "Stocks Tumble in Wild Trading." The following morning—the 25th—the* Tribune *gave the grim facts in the first paragraphs of two special articles. The first, by Fred Harvey, came from New York: the second, by William Shinnick, was local.*

RECORD SLUMP CHECKED:
KEY STOCKS RALLY

New York, Oct. 24—[Special]—Big bankers put a period to the most disastrous day in Wall Street history this afternoon by rushing first aid to the stock market, crushed and bleeding at every pore. . . . .

Sales for the day totaled 12,880,900, a new high record

for all time. The former record was 8,246,740 shares set on March 26 last.

Total losses cannot be accurately calculated because of the large number of markets and the thousands of securities not listed on any exchange. However, they were staggering, easily running into the billions of dollars. Fear struck the hearts of big speculators and little ones, big investors and little ones. Thousands threw their holdings into the whirling stock exchange for what they would bring. Losses were tremendous and thousands of prosperous brokerage and bank accounts, sound and healthy a week ago, were wrecked in the strange debacle, caused primarily by a combination of circumstances, but accelerated into a crash of fear. . . . .

CHICAGO TAKES MARKET LOSSES
WITHOUT MOAN

Chicagoans took their losses in yesterday's stock market battle like soldiers and like ladies and gentlemen.

Thousands of them fell before the fire of brokers' clerks demanding margins. Either they could not or would not expend any more money, their own precious ammunition, in shooting for profits that were too well hidden. Others played the string out to the end and were still, after a long downswing of prices in the morning and a later rally, standing by their stocks last night and hoping for better things. . . . .

⟨ *The market crash leads to a depression far worse than anyone imagined on October 25, 1929, but somehow Charles B. Pike raised money—not as much as had been hoped, but enough for the building on which he had set his heart. On February 10, 1932, it stood in Lincoln Park, nearing comple-*

*tion. With the smell of wet plaster everywhere, and the
noise of hammers ringing through the empty rooms, the
governing members gather for their annual meeting.*

The Seventy-Fifth Annual Meeting of the Chicago Historical Society was held in the Chicago Room of the Society's
new building in Lincoln Park, Wednesday, February 10, 1932,
at 3 o'clock. . . . .

Mr. Charles B. Pike submitted the following President's
report for the year:

"Ladies and Gentlemen: The Seventy-Fifth Annual Meeting
has been inaugurated by the gavel made from wood of old
Fort Dearborn. It was unfortunate that we could not have a
more fitting celebration to commemorate this event, but we
are all more interested, I think, in seeing the new building
than in anything else. Therefore, we are omitting reading
most of the reports.

"I think everyone will agree with me that finances are,
in these so-called days of financial and market depression,
the most important thing we have to contend with at this time.
As you know, we started our campaign for funds three days
after the crash of the market in 1929, so that the money which
has been contributed has been given through more than usual
generosity on the part of the subscribers. There have been
one hundred and ninety-five contributors to the Building &
Endowment Fund. The contributions total $887,287.00. The
largest is $50,000 and the smallest $1.00, while the average is
$4,300. Seventy contributors have paid their pledges in full.
In other words, we have received the sum of $184,812.00.
The total amount due on the second installment which was
called February 1 was $188,471.69. There has been paid on

the second installment $90,153.03, that is, more money pro
rata on every subscription than was paid last year, and I think
that at the end of the month practically all this second installment will be in.

"There is still due on the 1931 call $3,186.67, on the
1932, $98,318.66, on the 1933, the largest amount, $143,-
616.44, on the 1934, $83,388.17, and on the 1935, $91,763.33.
It is fortunate that these balances were in installments for
otherwise some of the subscribers would have found it difficult to pay.

"The whole problem as far as the building is concerned
is whether these pledges are good or not, and in view of the
facts, I think they are good. . . . ."

*By the fall of 1932 the building was finished, and the
installation of exhibits far enough advanced to give reporters
a preview. To the* Herald & Examiner, *the new museum is
nothing less than a historical wonder.*

"Five Centuries of Progress" might properly be the name
of an extraordinary exposition which is about to be opened
in Lincoln Park, not for a season or two, but for all time.

The Chicago Historical Society, whose subject is not
merely Chicago but the whole United States "from discovery
to recovery," granted a preview of the wonders of its new
museum at Clark St. and North Ave. yesterday to a small
group of newspaper people who were invited to tell the public what they saw.

It can't be done. Not in one day. Not in one newspaper.
What can be told, however, is that the show is one of the
finest things Chicago possesses, that it is a show which never

can be duplicated anywhere else, and that—for a student who knows how to use it—it is a university.

At a cost of about $1,000,000—not a dollar of it derived from taxation—the Society has at last obtained a worthy housing for its literally priceless treasures, the building itself, done in the Georgian Colonial tradition, being in itself an exhibit.

President Charles B. Pike of the Society and L. Hubbard Shattuck, director of the museum, acted as guides yesterday and explained the orderly arrangement.

"The scheme we have adopted," said Mr. Shattuck, "is a chronological presentation, so that a visitor, if he follows the prescribed path, can walk through the centuries and watch the unfolding of the nation's story."

You start with the discovery of America and you see an anchor which was used by Columbus himself. It is the gift of the Spanish people to Chicago's 1893 World's Fair and a gift from that fair to the Historical Society. . . . .

Thirty-eight rooms, many of them huge, house thirty-eight divisions of the epic story which the building as a whole tells.

There is the room devoted to the French explorers, there is the British colonial room, there is the later colonial reception room duplicating the Senate Chamber in the old congressional hall at Philadelphia. There you will see garments worn by President Washington at his second inaugural.

Then you pass through the Washington room, with intimate relics of the first President, through the New Republic room, where the influence of the French empire period dominates, through the Western room—depicting the march of the new nation across the continent, with scenes of the

⟨ Charles F. Gunther,
whose collection the Society
bought in 1920.

⟨ The entourage of Queen Marie of Romania arriving
at the Society on November 14, 1926. Despite the
weather, the Trustees perspired freely.

❴ *Laying the cornerstone, July 23, 1931: I. Newton Perry, Director L. Hubbard Shattuck, and Dr. Otto L. Schmidt.*

❴ *Laying the cornerstone: President Charles B. Pike spreads the mortar.*

([*The new building as it looked in October, 1931.*

([*The official opening,*
November 12, 1932:
Charles B. Pike,
Mrs. Lessing Rosenthal,
Dr. Otto L. Schmidt,
George W. Dixon,
Edward L. Glaser,
Frank J. Loesch.

⟨ *Princess Leilavanthi of Mysore*
viewing one of the
Thorne Miniature Rooms.

⟨ *Sally Rand and the fans*
that were always in the way.

❰ *"The mighty Gabby had hit a home run. The Cubs were in first place!*
Gabby, though he didn't know it, was in a museum."

❰ *An outstanding exhibition: Original cartoons of John T. McCutcheon.*
Mrs. John Lord King, John T. McCutcheon, and Mrs. John T. McCutcheon
at the opening, October 31, 1943.

(*"Four score and seven years ago . . . . ": November 19, 1950.*
Above, Governor Adlai E. Stevenson, Mayor Martin H.
Kennelly, Society President William McCormick Blair.
Below, a fascinated youngster, Linda Reed,
at the Gettysburg Address exhibit.

❪ Viscount Halifax, British Ambassador to the United States, and Lady Halifax visit the Society, with President Joseph M. Cudahy, May 11, 1941.

❪ The War of 1812 Room at 6:00 p. m. on Sunday, November 14, 1954. The dejected Director, Paul M. Angle, surveys the ruins.

(*The War of 1812 Room
five months after it was
destroyed by fire.
At left, one of the
special exhibits
installed for the
Society's Centennial:
Costumes of
a century ago.*

Mexican War, the California gold rush, the steel tenacles of the railroads reaching across deserts and over mountains.

You come to a great hall in which the Civil War is made vivid, one side devoted to the North, the other to the South, with a cracked old marble table in the center—the table on which peace was signed.

Marvellously ingenious tricks have been done to make the past seem alive. The great Chicago fire flames before your eyes and you can't imagine how it ever was put out. The city's first big tavern is shown, gay with lights. You can visit the 1893 World's Fair and think you are actually in it. Or, dipping deeper into the past, you can feel that you are running hopelessly from the Indians at Fort Dearborn.

Even the World War, in which 1,100 Chicago boys were killed, is adequately presented, and you can see a photograph of every one of them.

These are merely a few of the exhibits. For the serious student there are still greater treasures in the library, one of the finest of all historical libraries.

The museum is not yet open to the public. For the 2,800 members of the Society there will be a preview on October 9. The opening date for the public is November 1.

The members of the Society have their first look at the new building on October 9. Judith Cass, in the Tribune, *reports the event.*

Although the reception which the trustees of the Chicago Historical Society gave yesterday afternoon in the handsome new Georgian colonial building in Lincoln Park was simple, informal, and lacking in most of the adornments that dress up the average affair, the guests who filed past the receiving line from 3 until close to 6 o'clock found themselves at one of the most festive and intriguing parties ever given in Chicago.

The committee in charge refrained from the use of floral decorations which ordinarily lend atmosphere to the opening of a new building. There was atmosphere enough in the beautiful structure itself and in the wealth of historic treasures it houses. The only flowers in evidence were in the bouquet which Mrs. Charles B. Pike, wife of the president of the Society, held. The bouquet, which was sent to Mrs. Pike by Mrs. Robert G. McGann, was a prim old fashioned one of tightly wedged tea roses, sweet peas, and carnations against a round paper fringe—just the sort of floral offering which an early Chicago belle would have loved.

Mr. and Mrs. Pike headed the receiving line at the entrance to the foyer, which is a reproduction of Independence Hall in Philadelphia. Assisting them at intervals were Mr. and Mrs. Potter Palmer and Mr. and Mrs. Charles S. Dewey. Mrs. Pike wore a beige tunic dress and matching hat; Mrs. Palmer wore a black satin afternoon dress and a black turban with a twisted band of red, and Mrs. Dewey was in brown with a sable scarf.

The guests wandered through the rooms hunting former possessions of their ancestors, tracing families down through history, and viewing some of their own gifts to the Historical Society.

George Henry High, just back from a summer in the East, was explaining to friends in the Victorian room that the rosewood furniture, considered to be one of the most perfect examples of its kind in existence, had been given by his wife.

Originally the property of Mrs. High's grandmother, Mrs. Tuthill King, the lovely mellowed old pieces were brought to Chicago by boat in 1834, and miraculously survived the Chicago fire.

On the mantel in the same room is a gold and bronze clock and a pair of candelabra given to the late Dr. Charles C. Spencer by King Edward VII, then Prince of Wales, and inscribed, "In memory of three very pleasant days on the western plains." They were recently given to the Society by Dr. Spencer's daughter, Mrs. Eliphalet W. Cramer.

The guests, many of whose families have been affiliated with Chicago since the days of its early youth, included Mr. and Mrs. Arthur Meeker, who returned a few days ago from their summer stay in California; Mr. and Mrs. Charles W. Dempster, Mrs. Frederick T. Haskell, Mr. and Mrs. Samuel T. Chase, Mr. and Mrs. Albert Blake Dick, Mrs. Chauncey B. Borland, Mr. and Mrs. Barrett Wendell, Mr. and Mrs. Scott S. Durand, Mr. and Mrs. Ambrose C. Cramer, Mrs. Frederick W. Upham, Dr. Otto L. Schmidt, whose collection of furniture from early pioneer days is assembled in the Early Pioneer room; Mrs. John W. Gary, Mrs. Kersey Coates Reed, Mrs. Jacob Baur, Miss Nancy Taylor, Col. and Mrs. William N. Pelouze, Mrs. Dexter Fairbank, and Mr. and Mrs. B. Botsford Young.

On November 12, 1932, the Society opens its doors to the general public. Kathleen McLaughlin, writing in the Tribune, catches the spirit of the occasion.

Chicago's vibrant museum of its past, the new Chicago Historical building in Lincoln Park, was opened to the public yesterday in a brief ceremony in the tempo of the present. Charles B. Pike, president, officiated at a service before the entrance that was long on dignity but short on oratory.

Officials of the organization gathered at the Racquet Club preliminary to the program, and rode the short distance to the southwest corner of Lincoln Park. In the expanse before the main entrance a detachment of the Black Horse troop, in their dashing uniforms of black and gleaming white, ranged themselves on either side of the driveway to form a guard of honor through which the group proceeded to the portico.

The trustees then formed in a semi-circle behind President Pike who made the formal dedication in a few sentences, and then turned and unlocked the doors, entering with the official group.

"We stand here today at the portals of a building expressive of its purpose," he said in part, "ready to open it to the public. We are looking through the trees of Lincoln Park to the waters of Lake Michigan and Saint-Gaudens' statue of the Great Emancipator.

"When we enter we shall see the hat he wore, the scarf he wrapped around his shoulders, the coat he was assassinated in, and many other personal effects. Lincoln belongs to the ages. So also do Columbus and Washington. Housed in this building are relics of all of them, and many others who influenced the shaping of America's destinies. Permit me to congratulate the trustees in finishing this great work prior to the centennial of our city. And now, asking for guidance from on high in the conduct of this educational and patriotic enterprise, we open its doors."

Miss Rhea Zugenbuehler, of 1701 South 3rd Street, Maywood, was the first to pay admission to enter the galleries.

Mondays, Wednesdays, and Fridays are to be free days at the museum, but 25 cents is charged on other days of the week. . . . .

Among those prominent in yesterday's exercises were, Dr. Otto L. Schmidt, a past president; George W. Dixon, Frank Loesch, Joseph T. Ryerson, Potter Palmer, representing the Art Institute; Prof. Philip Fox, representing the Planetarium, and Stephen Simms, director of the Field Museum.

❨ *News items of the day make the Society's achievement in raising money for a new building look like a miracle.*

WARNS "HUNGER MARCHERS"
CITY CAN'T FEED THEM

A warning that funds of the Illinois Emergency Relief Commission, or relief agencies dependent upon it for support, will not be available to feed and lodge 300 "hunger marchers" who are scheduled to arrive in Chicago on Nov. 4 en route to Washington, was issued yesterday by Ald. James B. Waller [43d], chairman of the city council unemployment committee.

Ald. Waller added that the request for gas and oil for 24 trucks carrying a contingent of 200 Chicago "hunger marchers" who plan to join the transient group will be denied. Both requests were presented by representatives of the unemployed council.

HOLD OUT HOPE FOR 37¢ ON DOLLAR
BY MIDDLE WEST

Hope for the recovery of 37 cents on the dollar by holders of a $40,000,000 issue of serial gold notes in Middle

West Utilities Company is contained in a comprehensive report on the condition of the Insull holding concern issued yesterday by the noteholders' committee, headed by Charles S. Dewey.

STOCK PRICES AT CLOSING, NOV. 12

Am Tel & Tel	112¼	Repub Steel	8½
Bethlehem Stl	19⅞	Sears Roeb	22⅛
Chrysler	17	Std Oil Cal	27
Du Pont	39½	Std Oil N J	32⅞
Gen Elec	18⅛	Un Carbide	26
Gen Mot	15¼	Unit Aircraft	28⅛
Montgom Ward	14⅛	U S Gypsum	24¾
Nat Lead	65	U S Rubber	6½
Pac G & El	28⅝	U S Steel	39¼
Peoples Gas	74	Westingh El & M	31½
Phelps Dodge	6¾		

THE

MODERN

SOCIETY

1932 — 1956

❨ THE new building aggravates financial problems arising from the continuing depression. President Pike reports the gloomy truth at the annual meeting, October 10, 1934.

The regular October meeting of the Trustees of the Chicago Historical Society was held in the office of the President in the Society's building at 4 o'clock on Wednesday, October 10. . . . .

The President, Mr. Pike, prefaced his report by referring to the fact that on November 22 he will have completed seven years as President of the Society, and that October 10 marks the seventh anniversary of Mr. Shattuck's coming to the Society as Director. The President said that he felt it would be opportune to review the financial situation of the Society during the above period. He pointed out that from 1929 to 1931 the Society's income was about $42,000 a year, that due to business conditions this amount has been reduced by approximately $10,000 a year. The Society's income for 1933 was $33,517 and it is expected that the income for the current year will run about $32,000. . . . .

Membership dues show a decrease from $22,000 in 1928 to $10,500 in 1933. The Life Membership Endowment Fund has increased in the same period from $80,000 to $134,745. This accounts for some of the shrinkage in membership dues

209

because a concerted effort was made a few years ago to increase the Life Membership Endowment Fund. Many of the members who were paying annual dues took out Life Memberships. This, naturally, decreased the annual income and increased the Life Membership Endowment Fund.

On June 30, 1934, bonds and mortgages held by the Society were in default as to principal $71,850 and as to interest $5,003. It is hoped, however, that some of these mortgages and bonds will be restored since in several cases reorganization plans are being successfully carried out.

While the income has thus been decreasing, the operating costs of the Society have increased approximately $18,000 a year in the new building which is four times the size of the Society's old building at Dearborn and Ontario streets. The Society, nevertheless, has been run with the very strictest economy and has lived well within the approved budget each year and expects to effect further savings on the 1934 budget approved by the Trustees on January 10, 1934. It has been necessary, however, for the Society to draw on funds from the Building and the General Endowment Funds to meet operating expenses, but this was considered better policy than to increase the bank loan which now stands at $5,000.

In discussing the situation regarding pledges to the Building and Endowment Fund, the President reported that there had been collected to date $723,118. There is still $169,769 outstanding as of October 10 which includes $63,000 due in 1935. It is estimated that of this total of unpaid pledges, approximately $150,000 are of doubtful value. We expect a substantial payment on the last installment of the pledges due in February 1935. Out of these funds the Society should be able to retire the outstanding balance of $5,325.76 due the architects and the present bank loan. In view of present business conditions the President considered the payment of 81% of the pledges before the final due date as an indication of the excellent quality of these pledges. Every effort will be made to collect as much of the balance due as possible and he pointed out that plans must be inaugurated to increase both the capital and the income of the Society. Mr. Pike recommended that the Trustees make every possible effort to assist the Society to increase its income by securing new Members. . . . .

In summarizing the financial situation from the standpoint of the Society's development and general progress during the past seven years, the President pointed out that it had been able to secure a fine site in Lincoln Park, the value of which can hardly be estimated in dollars and cents, it has secured pledges to the amount of $892,888 and a new building which if erected under present conditions could not be duplicated for less than $1,000,000. . . . .

❲ *Mrs. James Ward Thorne opens a notable exhibit that will delight visitors to the Society for the next several years.*

Several hundred interested Chicagoans were initiated into the glamorous world of miniature yesterday [December 16, 1934] when Mrs. James Ward Thorne, speaking in the auditorium of the Chicago Historical Society as a preface to the formal opening of her miniature room exhibit, told them how she collected the tiny furnishings of the 27 rooms.

"In my collecting," she said, "I adhere to only one rule. When I see something I want, I buy it then and there. If I don't, it's always gone when I go back."

This rule was learned, she said, in an arduous tour of many European countries, including Italy, where on the banks of the Tiber she purchased the tiny Venetian chandeliers which started her on what she termed "the road to exhaustion". . . . .

In the course of her lecture she imparted some of her secrets. In her 1885 kitchen, for instance, what appear to be golden brown doughnuts in the cooky jars were once toy automobile tires, and their coating is not sugar, but soda. An entrancing bust in the Louis XVI salon is really a chess queen. The back of a carved Spanish bed is a Spanish comb. The convex mirror in the federal dining room was made from a watch crystal, and the white fur rug in the modernistic salon once was part of an ermine collar.

Most of the miniature furnishings, however, are genuine pieces, such as exquisite Staffordshire and Chelsea china, hall marked silver, Chinese porcelains and antique pewter and brasses.

From the lecture the spectators proceeded to the hall housing the miniature rooms, emerging some hours later in a daze, for, like Alice in Wonderland, they had lost all sense of size.*

⟨ *A Dallas editor makes an admission—rare for a Texan—that his city could learn something from Chicago. His article appeared in the October 20, 1938 issue of the* Dallas News.

. . . . The Dallas Historical Society is offering Dallas an opportunity to participate in the creation of a Texas museum

---

* *The Thorne Miniature Rooms may now be seen at the Art Institute.*

of the sort that has proven popular and profitable to other progressive cities.

A substantial beginning has been made by public-spirited citizens who are ambitious to preserve for the future the story of Texas' glorious past as it is expressed in literature, dress, household arts and artifacts that reflect the customs of the pioneers and preserve the traditions of our ancestors. . . . .

If one questions the civic value of historical museums he has but to visit some of the progressive cities which possess such attractions and note the interest and affection with which residents and visitors regard them.

The Chicago Historical Society's Museum of American History is a notable example of what Dallas, in a limited way and with a late start, may be able, in time, to do with a museum of Texas history.

Armed with a letter of introduction from Herbert Gambrell, director of the Dallas Museum, a party of Dallas residents recently had the privilege of inspecting the Chicago museum with its director, L. H. Shattuck. They had thought to spend an hour or so, but remained most of the day and left reluctantly because of another engagement.

Of course, their interest was intrigued by such treasures as the doors from the house in which Columbus once lived, the anchor from his ship Santa Maria, a bottle of tea leaves from the Boston Tea Party, the suit Washington wore at his second inaugural, the desk he used as commander of the colonial army, the clock given him by Frederick the Great, Martha's sewing box and dinner bell, Lee's clock, Grant's saddle, the lantern from Fort Sumter, Dewey's loving cup, the coat Lincoln wore when assassinated, his hat, umbrella and shawl, and Mrs. Lincoln's piano.

Not interested in such things? Hundreds of thousands are. What to you may be trivial are to them proofs of struggle, strife, endeavor, achievement. They are the physical confirmation of America's written history and an inspiration to patriotism and good citizenship.

In 1937 the Chicago museum had 160,162 visitors. Not so many considering Chicago's size, you think, but the museum was founded in 1856 and most Chicago residents saw it several times before 1937. Presumably most of these 160,162 were nonresidents, visitors in the city eager to see something they could remember with pleasure the remainder of their lives.

The Chicago museum has been built by public contributions of money and exhibits. During 1937 it received more than 2,500 separate gifts. Cash gifts since its foundation have totaled $779,700.85 with additional pledges on hand of $112,-887.15.

The Chicago Historical Society is a private organization depending for its existence upon income from memberships, door fees and endowment without any revenue from city or county, yet, of all Chicago's institutions, it is probably doing most to promote patriotic, civic and educational interests of the city. Its operating expenses in 1937 were approximately $70,000.

Any description of the Chicago museum deserves more space than is available here. It is the most modern museum of its kind. It is not a mummy case in which remains are well preserved but seldom seen. It does not inter its relics in dreary glass cases but has breathed new life into its collections by reproducing their original settings. If you ever go to Chicago you ought to visit it. It's worth your time.

Another October visitor—Mrs. Eleanor Roosevelt—is favorably impressed, and devotes one of her "My Day" columns to the Society.

CHICAGO . . . . Mrs. Cotsworth and Mrs. Flynn kindly asked an extremely interesting woman, Miss Harriet Vittum, head of the Northwestern University Settlement, to have breakfast with us this morning. . . . .

After she left us, we drove up to the Chicago Historical Society. This, I am told, was started to preserve things of historical interest to Chicago, but has broadened into being a museum of American history. The exhibits are intriguingly arranged to show different periods of our history. As is natural in Illinois, this museum has a wonderful collection of things which relate to Abraham Lincoln. The Healy portrait seemed to me particularly fine, and the director of the museum told us Robert Todd Lincoln considered it the best likeness of his father.

I particularly liked the head done by Gutzon Borglum, a strong and massive head, with a mouth which always seems to me very sensitive. I am inclined to think Massey's interpretation of Lincoln's character in the new play, "Abe Lincoln in Illinois," is probably correct. It was a complicated personality, often at war with itself.

I found the reproduction of the Lincoln parlor in Springfield and the reproduction of the room in which he died exceptionally interesting. We were told the dimensions of the cabin in which he was born and the room in which he died were identical, so at the beginning and end of his life he was in touch with bare simplicity. I think this phase of life was never out of his mind, even in his moments of greatest success and glory. We also saw Mrs. Thorne's miniature rooms, a triumph of delicate art, and most interesting to the student of different periods of decoration and furniture.

A prize-winning group from the sales force of a packing company was going through the museum. They came from all over the country and I could not help thinking what a tremendous amount of history they would carry away after a morning spent in this environment.

❲ *The Society proves that it has no hidebound notions about the scope of history. Paul R. Allerup, International News Service, writes a story that almost matches the famous home run.*

CHICAGO, Nov. 3.—The mighty Casey who struck out may have to play second fiddle for posterity to the mighty Gabby who hit a home run.

The mighty Gabby, none other than Charles Leo Hartnett, the fellow who piloted Chicago's own Cubs to the 1938 National League baseball championship, hit his home run in the ninth inning of the Pittsburgh-Chicago game here on September 28.

The home run won the game for the Cubs and was the blow that more than any other single accomplishment clinched the title for Chicago.

Yesterday it was revealed the paraphernalia Gabby used in the game—his catching glove, mask, chest protector and shinguards, as well as the home run bat—have been given, upon request, to the Chicago Historical Society.

These exalted objects will soon go on display in the Society's museum, there to remind generations as yet unborn that Mudville's mighty Casey was a shoemaker compared to Chicago's mighty Gabby.

While it is pleasant to contemplate the reverence and awe with which the fans of the year 2038 may stand and gaze at these sacred relics of our own backward age, the thought comes that a glove, a bat, a chest protector, will not adequately tell the story of that historic moment on a September day in 1938, when 34,465 leading citizens of the time shouted themselves sick with excitement at the mighty Gabby's momentous feat.

We hope the museum will select one of the leading authors of our day to chronicle in stirring, complete terms, the story of that wonderous home run.

Remember? It had been a long game. The lead had changed hands several times. Finally, the ninth inning. The score was 5–5. The Cubs were at bat. As the sun fell behind the grandstand and darkness crept over the field, the Chicagos were making their last stand. They were half a game behind the first-place Pirates, but victory would boost them into the lead.

Up stepped Cub Number One—out! Cub Number Two —out! The officials looked over the dimming field. As Hartnett stepped up to bat it was generally agreed that the game would be called when the mighty Gabby made the third out. A tie game would hearten Pittsburgh, squelch the Cubs.

The mighty Gabby looked at the first pitch. Strike! Pitch number two—strike! The Cub cause seemed lost. Pitch number three—wham!

The mighty Gabby had hit a home run. The Cubs were in first place! Gabby, though he didn't know it, was in a museum.

❡ *Charles B. Pike died on April 26, 1941. To him, primarily, the Society owes its present building; to him, and to his brother and widow, it owes much of its financial stability. The Trustees, meeting on May 14, 1941, record Mr. Pike's services in a warmly worded memorial.*

. . . . The main interest in later life of Mr. Pike, and the one by which he will be remembered, was his service as a member, Trustee and Officer of the Chicago Historical Society. He was elected President on November 22, 1927, and served until his death on April 26, 1941, covering a period of nearly fourteen years, by far the longest service of any President of the Society.

His services as President began at a time when the Trustees of the Society were earnestly seeking to find a suitable location for the erection of a new building. The Trustees had long been considering such a change, in view of the inadequate space and fire hazards of the Society's building at Dearborn Avenue and Ontario Street, erected shortly after the great Chicago Fire.

The times were favorable for securing public subscriptions in the sum of over one million dollars in the hope that a suitable site would be found for the new building; but subsequent financial conditions made a very unfavorable time. Many of our pledges were defaulted. It was Mr. Pike's achievement that he completed the endowment to the extent necessary to secure the present site.

It was fortunate that Mr. Pike's personal and political affiliations were such that after much negotiation on the part of Mr. Pike and the Trustees with public officials, a permanent site in Lincoln Park was assured by legislative action respectively of the Lincoln Park Commission, the City Council of Chicago and the State Legislature of Illinois. Mr. Pike's next effort was to secure the erection of a suitable building in the new location. The architects generously donated their services. Mr. L. Hubbard Shattuck visited many museum and historical society buildings, and his reports to Mr. Pike, with the latter's personal knowledge in his avocation as an expert in museums, secured the construction of the present handsome structure, unique among similar buildings in the United States.

Mr. Pike had the well-deserved personal enjoyment of securing the erection of the building for about $100,000 less than the estimated cost when the contracts were being let.

His passion was to publicize the Historical Society. He wished the generation of children in our schools to visualize by its exhibits the glory of America and its individual opportunities and to create a patriotic pride in their native or acquired land. In this he was eminently successful, as has been proved by the many tens of thousands of children who have visited the building and profited thereby.

His wisdom in portraying history in chronological sequence has won the admiration of scholars and historians as well as the public at large. No other institution of this kind had ever before attempted this logical presentation of historical material. The Society has grown not only financially under his wise and vigorous leadership, but has increased greatly its educational standards and civic usefulness.

Through his sound judgment and broad concept in the management of the affairs of the Society, his generosity in contributing over $60,000,* his gift of one of the largest and

---

* *Mr. Pike's total benefactions far exceeded this figure.*

most outstanding collections of historical prints in the United States, as well as other valuable Americana, Charles Burrall Pike has achieved a position unparalleled in the history of this institution.

His absolute integrity and unswerving devotion to the Chicago Historical Society and its works, drew to him a host of friends who were ever ready to listen to his advocacy of any good cause. They knew that, unmindful of personal advantage, he was himself a generous giver of means as well as of time and energy; he asked of others only as he himself freely gave.

He was ever an optimist. In his orbit the world moved in the right direction always. He had ever a message for discouraged people, and, as regards the future growth and value of the Chicago Historical Society, certainly he had no misgivings.

His active mind, ever fresh and alert, his penetrating and incisive judgment, keen critical powers, quiet humor and singleness of purpose deeply impressed us all.

This tribute would be incomplete if we, as members of the Board of Trustees, did not add an expression of the deep personal sorrow felt by each one of us in the loss of our great leader and valued friend, whose relationship with us was always marked by cordiality, good will and understanding. It was our privilege and joy to work with him in the development of this institution, which will be a lasting and permanent memorial to his memory.

⟨ *The Society, with fitting ceremony, opens an exhibit which, in the fifteen years that have since elapsed, has interested and instructed hundreds of thousands of visitors.*

At 4:00 on the afternoon of Sunday, November 16, 1941, the new exhibit of twenty dioramas depicting Abraham Lincoln's life was formally opened by President Joseph M. Cudahy to the Society's members and the public. This opening culminated three years of construction and research to make these dioramas mechanically and historically correct.

In Mr. Cudahy's dedication speech, he expressed the Society's appreciation to the various Lincoln authorities in the Middle West whose valuable suggestions helped the Society achieve a high standard of historical accuracy. Mr. Cudahy also paid high praise to the supervisors and employees of the Museum Extension Program who built the exhibit. The people voluntarily worked overtime for several weeks in order to complete every detail before the November 16th dedication.

As President Cudahy cut the white satin ribbon leading into the diorama gallery, an organ in Lee Hall pealed forth with the "Battle Hymn of the Republic," followed by other musical selections of the Civil War period, some of which were favorites of Abraham Lincoln. One of the first Trustees to view these finished dioramas was Mrs. Charles B. Pike, whose husband, the late Charles B. Pike, was President of the Society when the first plans for the Lincoln dioramas were formed. Until the Museum closed at six o'clock that afternoon, members and visitors by the hundreds viewed the exhibit.

All members of the Society were invited to a reception given by Mr. and Mrs. Cudahy in the Senate Chamber at 4:30 o'clock. Presiding at the two tea tables were Mrs. James Ward Thorne, Mrs. Potter Palmer, Mrs. James M. Hopkins, Mrs. William McCormick Blair, Mrs. William R. Odell, Mrs. Arthur Meeker, Mrs. Patrick A. Valentine, Mrs. Charles

Garfield King, Mrs. Charles Dempster, Mrs. Cecil Barnes, Mrs. A. A. Carpenter, Mrs. Robert B. Gregory, and Mrs. Albert A. Sprague.

(*A fan dancer's press agent has an idea. The Director of the Society, like all men of his calling, is not averse to publicity for his institution. He gets it, in quantity. This, the* Herald American's *story, appears on May 9, 1943.*

SALLY LOSES FANS TO POSTERITY

The plumes which fanned Sally Rand to prosperity will be preserved for posterity.

The same world-famous fans, known from the halls of Montezuma to the shores of Tripoli as the symbol of the thin difference between one lady's art and another's, will be turned over to the Chicago Historical Society.

The idea was Sally's, it was announced yesterday. She thought, she said, the Society would be interested in keeping a memento of the Century of Progress Exposition, held in Chicago in 1933 and 1934. L. H. Shattuck, the scholarly, bespectacled director of the Society, explained:

"The fans made history. They represented one phase of American life, and help to round out the picture for the ages."

Until a week ago, Sally said, she used huge, 65-inch rubber balloons for her dances, a practice she followed since 1934. She said: "I used about 400 rubber balloons a year. But now they're gone, and you know how critical the rubber shortage is. The mortality rate of balloons in night clubs, crowded these days with soldiers and sailors, is very high."

Shattuck, somewhat awed, ventured the information that the shirt off the ostrich's back would be presented to the

Society Tuesday by the dancer herself. He felt the preservation of the fans represented a new trend in historical collection. He added:

"It means we're trying to get a broader view. Things we overlooked in the past are now becoming recognized as having a place in the historical picture of the world."

Those who remembered the fair agree with Shattuck that the fans were overlooked, but definitely.

The Trustees, however, decide that the Director—or maybe Sally—had gone too far. Jack McPhaul continues the story in the Chicago Times *of May 11.*

SALLY RAND FANS HER ANGER OVER FAN TRICK

Sally Rand, the little girl with the big fans, charged today that the Chicago Historical Society has played a "shabby trick" on her.

Originally, Sally had a date to journey to the Society's headquarters at North and Clark this afternoon and with fitting ceremonies present to the Society the pair of ostrich fans that a lot of folks credit with pulling Chicago's Century of Progress out of the red in 1933.

But Sally won't be keeping that date.

Headed by President Joseph M. Cudahy, the Society's board of trustees met yesterday. At its conclusion the board issued this statement for the press:

"The board feels that the fans used by Miss Sally Rand at A Century of Progress are not relative to the World's Columbian Exposition material now on exhibition and does not believe they have sufficient historical interest to warrant their acceptance by the museum."

These bleak words were a far cry from the jubilant press

release issued by the Society Saturday announcing that Sally and her fans would be welcomed with open arms (something Sally never dared on the lake front) and that Sally's ostrich protectors would be given a permanent place of record in the archives of Chicago's lusty history.

Who or what caused the Society's change of heart was a mystery, a mystery equal to the wonderment on the part of hundreds of thousands at the Fair's Streets of Paris as to what Sally had behind the fans.

Said Sally spiritedly: "This is a shabby trick to embarrass me. If I had sought publicity of this sort I would deserve to be knocked down. But I didn't start this. A representative of the Society got in touch with me and suggested I contribute the fans. I agreed. Later I saw newspaper stories telling about the presentation. The Society put those out, I didn't.

"I was all set to go out there when I learned that the Society had declined the gift. I telephoned the museum but couldn't find anyone to talk to. It seems to me they should have at least sent me a letter."

Sally makes her own contribution: so Jerry Thorp reports in the Daily News *of May 12.*

SALLY RAND PITCHES CURVES
TO FAN HISTORICAL SOCIETY

The sedate Chicago Historical Society is waving her fans, figuratively of course, just to grab some free space in the public prints, an offended and indignant Sally Rand opined today.

"Did I offer my fans to this society?" she asked between bites of a 2 p.m. breakfast in her room at the Hotel Sherman.

"No," was her own emphatic answer. "They asked for them and then had the gall to announce that they are not of sufficient historical interest." The last phrase was uttered with all the imitative smugness at her command.

[The curator's office of the Historical Society begs to differ with Miss Rand as to who originally thought the fans should be relegated to covering bare spots in museum show-cases. A press agent called the Society, the office reported, and volunteered the fans. At first, the office said, the idea seemed sound, but the Trustees thought otherwise—it was simply fanatical, they decided.]

"What is of historical interest from this dizzy decade?" the fiery-eyed dancer continued. "If I had a museum I'd have a flagpole that a flagpole sitter sat on. I'd have a goldfish that one of the college boys swallowed."

At this point the diminutive Miss Rand, who weighs a scant 105 pounds, sans fan, paused to reflect.

"But maybe I don't know what is of historical interest," she pondered. "I've never been to a historical museum."

Then brightly: "Have you?"

"No."

"No—of course not. And neither has anyone else I know. But that's the way it has been all my life. City officials, societies, and lots of others that couldn't get any publicity on their own have used me to get newspaper space. It's hurt me sometimes, but then I have to put up with it."

With machine-gun rapidity she was back on the original subject, the fans that fanned the turnstiles of the Chicago World's Fair as nothing else could fan them.

"I still have those fans and they make up part of my regular wardrobe—my stage wardrobe, of course. I can use them so what's the use of getting yourself in a history museum when you're still getting $2,500 a week for waving them around?"

Sally, who admits to 39 years but looks 30, even without makeup, tossed a blond wisp of hair behind her ear and looked dreamily out the window.

"I wonder," she meditated, "what that outfit would have done if Eve had offered them her fig leaf?"

Editorial writers the country over have a field day. The pithiest, and funniest, comment is that of David V. Felts in the Decatur Herald.

. . . . It is true, of course, that nobody was interested in seeing Sally's fans, even in 1933. They tried to see Sally and the fans were always in the way.

⟨ *In 1946 the Society reaches the age of ninety years— almost the limit for human beings, and not a common attainment for institutions. To mark the anniversary, President Joseph M. Cudahy issues a brief statement, and most of the Spring, 1946, issue of* Chicago History, *the Society's new quarterly, is given over to a concise history. We quote the first part of President Cudahy's statement, and the last section of the history.*

. . . . A ninetieth anniversary usually means quiet old age. The Chicago Historical Society, however, considers its ninety-year history a preparatory period for greater public service. It looks forward to changes in its museum that will convey a more vivid, more meaningful conception of the history of our country to a larger number of visitors; it contemplates improvements that will enable its library to render even more effective service both to scholars and the general public; it is desirous of enlarging its publication program; it seeks opportunities to increase the effectiveness of the educational work that it now carries on in coöperation with the public and parochial schools. . . . .

. . . . For fourteen years the Society has followed the pattern outlined by those who foresaw the greatly enlarged scope which a new building would give to its activities. Visitors in numbers undreamed of before 1932 have been attracted by its museum. Since that date more than a million schoolchildren have profited by it—as individual visitors, in classes, or as attendants at the Saturday morning lectures. The museum has not remained static. Timely exhibits have kept it in tune with a rapidly changing world, and ways to improve permanent exhibits have been sought constantly. Modern media of information have been used to keep its offerings before the public. The library has grown steadily, all the while serving a quiet though fundamentally important purpose as a repository of historical material and as a source of authoritative information about Chicago and the region of which it is the center. . . . .

Upon the death of Mr. Pike in 1941, Joseph M. Cudahy was elected to the Society's presidency. After the sudden death of L. Hubbard Shattuck in 1945, Paul M. Angle was appointed director. Under these officers and an energetic board of trustees, the Society is embarking upon the last decade of its first hundred years. Its goal is clear primacy among institutions of its kind. With public support, tendered in the spirit for which Chicago is famous, success is certain.

❡ *Comedy continues to intrude at fairly regular intervals. This time it takes the form of a bibulous robber with uncommon ingenuity in finding a hiding place. The* Tribune *tells the story on February 3, 1948.*

With the help of Abraham Lincoln's bed, Roger Anderson, 34, of 1533 Madison street, worked out quite a system for looting the Chicago Historical Society museum in Lincoln Park. His undoing was too much whisky.

Anderson was seized by Sgt. Frank Doyle and a squad of Racine av. police who were signaled by a motorman on a North av. street car at Damen av. Anderson was waving two pistols and bragging of his duels with western sheriffs.

One look at the pistols—E. Whitneys, calibers .31 and .36, circa 1846—convinced police that Anderson had been rooting in an antique cabinet. Questioning disclosed it had been in the museum.

Anderson said he visited the museum during the afternoon, shortly before closing time, and hid beneath Lincoln's bed.* After everyone had left the building he went to the gunroom and smashed one of the cases, removing the Whitneys and another comparatively modern pistol.

"In February last year I did the same thing," Anderson confessed. "That time I got $33 and a typewriter."

He sold one pistol to an antique shop for $4 and spent the money on drinks before getting on the street car.

Dr. Alfred F. Hopkins, museum curator, was nettled at Anderson's lack of taste. "Among the 75 weapons on display are a good many that are choice collector's items, worth a

---

* *In fact, the bed on which Lincoln spent the last hours of his life, from the boardinghouse opposite Ford's Theater.*

good deal of money," he said. "Those Anderson took are standard pieces. They won't even fire, since the springs have been removed. I assure you that from now on we'll check to see who is lurking under Lincoln's bed."

❨ *A news item, dated December 16, 1948, chronicles an important step in the progress of the Society.*

Though feminine members of the Chicago Historical Society long have been a guiding force in the creation of the Society's invaluable museum of treasures, they have waited 91 years before finally creating their own organization. William Mc-Cormick Blair, president of the Society, today announces the formation of a women's group, to be known as the Guild of the Society. The Guild, with the first meeting set for Jan. 24 in the Historical Society building in Lincoln Park, will further activities of the Society in vividly unfolding historic annals through exhibitions.

Mrs. James M. Hopkins, whose late husband was for many years vice president of the Society, has been chosen Guild chairman, and Mr. Blair's sister, Mrs. Howard Linn, is vice chairman. Mrs. Richard I. Stearns is secretary-treasurer, and on the board of directors are Mrs. Blair, Mrs. Stanley Keith, Mrs. Philip K. Wrigley, Mrs. Joseph M. Cudahy, whose late husband preceded Mr. Blair as president; Mrs. James Ward Thorne, Mrs. Charles Garfield King, whose son is a member of the board of trustees; Mrs. Richard T. Crane, Mrs. Stuyvesant Peabody, and Mrs. Joseph T. Ryerson.

Mrs. Peabody's late husband was a member of the Society's board of trustees, as was the late Mr. Ryerson, who is remembered as one of the Society's most generous donors.

❲ *The Society offers the most unusual—and to many visitors the most moving—exhibits of its long history. The record is from* Chicago History, *Fall, 1950.*

On Sunday, November 19, 1950, exactly four score and seven years after Abraham Lincoln began his dedicatory remarks at Gettysburg with those very words, the Chicago Historical Society unveiled the five copies of the address which he is known to have written. Owned by three institutions and one individual, these documents had never before been brought together. Sheathed in Lucite, standing vertically in a beautiful museum case guarded by two motionless soldiers, they presented a sight which few visitors will ever forget.

Three hundred chairs which had been placed in Lincoln Hall were filled long before 3:00 p.m., when William McCormick Blair, President of the Society, called for order. With the audience standing in silence, a color guard from Fort Sheridan presented the flag of the United States. Mr. Blair then introduced Martin H. Kennelly, Mayor of Chicago. . . . .

Following Mayor Kennelly, Mr. Blair presented Adlai E. Stevenson, Governor of Illinois. . . . .

At the conclusion of Governor Stevenson's remarks the audience stood in silence while a bugler sounded taps. The color guard retired the colors, and the meeting adjourned.

One week later—on Sunday, November 26—two of the country's foremost Lincoln authorities spoke in the Society's auditorium on the significance of the Gettysburg Address. Benjamin P. Thomas, author of *Lincoln's New Salem, Portrait for Posterity*, and *Theodore Dwight Weld*, took for his subject, "The Meaning of the Gettysburg Address, Then and Today," while Roy P. Basler, author of *The Lincoln Legend* and editor of the new edition of Lincoln's writings now being compiled under the auspices of the Abraham Lincoln Association, spoke on the theme, "An Appreciation of the Gettysburg Address". . . . .

The Gettysburg Address Exhibit lasted twelve days, from November 19 through November 30. During that period approximately 10,000 people saw the five original documents. Few of that number, we believe, will ever forget the experience. Most visitors took time to read all five manuscripts, and the intensity of their interest was indicated by their obvious absorption and by their hushed voices.

From a superficial point of view, the assembling and exhibiting of these five great documents on the "four score and seven year" anniversary of their origin might seem to be merely a clever device to obtain publicity and increase attendance. If that had been our only purpose, we could certainly say that we had succeeded. But our fundamental aim went far beyond these shallow objectives: we hoped, by this dramatic means, to recall to large numbers the present-day importance of that democratic creed that Lincoln formulated so superbly at Gettysburg. How well we succeeded in this purpose none can tell.

We know that all who saw the Gettysburg Address exhibit share our gratitude to the owners of the documents— the Library of Congress, the Illinois State Historical Library, the Cornell University Library, and the Hon. Oscar B. Cintas —for permitting them to be displayed at the Society.

❲ *At the ninety-sixth annual meeting the members of the Society adopt a memorial to a former Trustee, a munificent benefactor, and a great lady.*

When Mrs. Joseph M. Cudahy died at Palm Beach, Florida, on April 7, 1953, the Chicago Historical Society lost a friend, supporter, and worker whose place no one will ever fill.

To the Society Mrs. Cudahy gave, first of all, her intense and sustained interest. During her husband's presidency she shared with him, though unobtrusively, the responsibilities of administration, and came to know the inner workings of the organization as intimately as any Trustee or staff member. With interest went a willingness to face the problems, sometimes distressing, that occur in every group of human beings, and to bring her unexcelled good sense to their solution.

After her husband's death in 1947 Mrs. Cudahy became, somewhat reluctantly, a member of the Board of Trustees. Thereafter, in her capacity as Chairman of the Museum Committee, she added lavish amounts of her time to the interest from which the Society had long benefited. There were few weeks in which she did not spend hours in the building, conferring with the Director and Museum Curator on exhibits, going over recent acquisitions, and planning activities. In this field her special talents—knowledge of fine furniture and the decorative arts, cultivated taste, a flair for dramatic presentation, and innate good judgment—were invaluable.

Soon after becoming a member of the Board of Trustees, Mrs. Cudahy took the lead in organizing the Guild of the Chicago Historical Society, and while she refused to accept an executive office in the organization, she helped to shape its course during the first years of its existence. The success of this fine women's group, and the benefits that it has already conferred upon the Society, are further testimony to the effectiveness of her service.

Finally, Mrs. Cudahy gave liberally and unselfishly of her means to the Society. During Mr. Cudahy's presidency she started the practice of making a substantial annual contribution, and continued it until her death. It was characteristic of her to stipulate that the funds she provided should be used for such undramatic purposes as the restoration of paintings, the repair of prints, or the purchase of a badly needed carpet, rather than for more striking ends that might appeal to other donors. Beyond money went her willingness to donate her own cherished possessions, in china, silver, glass, or furniture, when something she herself owned was needed for a Society exhibition. Our gratitude for her generosity during these years loses nothing in the face of the extremely generous provision that she made for the Society in her will.

Our regret at the loss of Mrs. Cudahy as a co-worker is deepened by the sorrow which her death has brought to us all. A friend of some members of the Board at the time of her election, she quickly endeared herself to those whom she had not previously known. The memory of her gracious personality, her unfailing kindness, and her unaffected friendliness will not fade with the passing years.

Realizing, as we do, that words cannot adequately express our feelings, we nevertheless place this memorial statement on the permanent records of the Chicago Historical Society.

❴ *On Monday morning, November 15, 1954, front-page headlines announce disaster: "MUSEUM FIRE! HINT ARSON" and "$100,000 MUSEUM FIRES RUIN HISTORIC COLLECTIONS." We quote the* Tribune's *account.*

Simultaneous fires damaged valuable relics yesterday afternoon in two rooms of the Chicago Historical Society, North av. at Clark st. in Lincoln Park. Director Paul M. Angle said the damage will be at least $100,000.*

Firemen were extinguishing flames in the Victorian room, at the northwest corner, when they learned they were also needed in the War of 1812 room, at the southwest corner. Both rooms are on the main floor of the building.

"Some of our finest paintings in both rooms apparently have been destroyed," said Angle, who said there was also damage to fine Victorian furniture. He said both rooms were "a mess," and that close inspection would be necessary before the extent of the damage could be determined. The heaviest damage apparently was in the War of 1812 room.

The fires were listed as being of "suspicious origin" by Chief Arthur Schmid of the 3d battalion, whose damage estimate, ignoring historical value, was $25,000.

Schmid said that both fires had apparently been touched off by holding matches at the base of window draperies. Schmid and his men had answered a telephone alarm and were busy in the Victorian room when the blaze in the War of 1812 room was discovered. Between 75 and 100 persons were in the museum when the fires broke out.

Fire Atty. Earle Downes started an investigation.

---

* *An overestimate. Damage amounted to approximately $65,000, of which $40,000 was recovered from insurance. But several fine paintings were completely destroyed.*

The painting, "The Battle of Plattsburg," by Alonzo Chappel was destroyed and the following paintings were among those seared and blistered by the flames: "The Capture of the American Flotilla on Lake Borgne," by T. L. Hornbrook; "Henry Clay," by George Cooke; "The Battle of Lake Erie," by Ambrose Garneray; "Stephen Decatur," by an unidentified painter; "Charles Burrall Pike," by Sir William Orpen; "Joshua Barney," by Chappel; and "Miss Honora Sneyde," by George P. A. Healy. Other portraits suffered heat damage. Period furniture, pianos, drapes, candelabra, tables, sculpture, and a huge ornate glass chandelier all suffered fire damage.

The Society recovers from disaster in exactly five months. Its own release announces the reopening of the rooms.

The Chicago Historical Society will reopen on Friday, April 15, the two galleries that were devastated by fire on November 14, 1954.

Paul M. Angle, director, announced that both rooms—the Victorian Parlor and the War of 1812 Room—have been restored to their former beauty through the patience and skill of America's finest craftsmen and the donation of treasured heirlooms by members of the Society.

"Damaged furniture that looked like a complete loss has been restored so expertly that not even a trained eye can detect repairs and replacements," he said. "Several paintings that appeared to be hurt irreparably have been saved at no cost in appearance."

The initial conclusion that the fires were set by an arsonist has not been dispelled, Angle said, and the crime so far is unsolved. The Society, he added, is taking the most effective measures possible to prevent a similar disaster in the future.

Two other galleries—the Westward Expansion Room and the New Republic Room—closed since the fire for redecoration for smoke damage, also will be reopened.

The War of 1812 Room, which suffered the greatest destruction in the fire, has a number of new acquisitions. Inspired by the famous Blue Room in the White House, it now has a White House mantel that was presented to the Society by the Commission of the Executive Mansion, Washington, D. C., in 1951. The draperies are an exact copy of those hanging in the White House Blue Room. Several valuable oil paintings, a watercolor, a pair of brass andirons, a pair of Empire style candelabra, and a copper spike from the U.S.S. *Constitution* ("Old Ironsides") made by Paul Revere in Boston in 1798 have been added to this restored period room.

The furniture in the Victorian Parlor has been skillfully restored. The draperies, after considerable research, were expertly copied from American designs of the Victorian period. Goldleaf cornices now ornament the windows and several articles of decoration have been added to the room to enhance its attractiveness.

❡ *Over the years the Society has received a great many gifts, some of them very large in amount. None, however, was ever given in finer spirit than the donation acknowledged in the following article from the Fall, 1955, issue of* Chicago History.

Nine years ago we employed Charles Johnson on our museum staff. We did so with considerable reluctance, for we do not ordinarily hire people at the age of seventy-eight. But

Johnson was tough, wiry, and active—a bantam-rooster kind of man; he looked ten years younger than he was; and he wanted to work. Moreover, he was skillful with his hands, and we needed help. He explained that he was a widower, that he had no dependents, and that he needed only a small salary.

We expected that Charlie would be with us for a few months, or a year or two at most. But year after year passed, and he was on the job every day. From the beginning, he earned his salary, and he won and held the affection of all who knew him.

Two or three years ago age began to take its toll, even from the Charlie Johnson whom we had come to think of as indestructible. Several illnesses sent him to the hospital. Every time we thought we would never see him again, but he always came back, able and anxious to work. He knew that he was approaching the end, and he hoped that it would come while he was at the Society and working.

In that he was to be disappointed. Late in May he left work, ill. On June 19 he died at the hotel where he had lived with his brother.

At the time of Charlie's death we were holding a pay check and cash totalling $75.00. We notified his brother, Raymond Johnson, that we would pay the amount at any time to him or to anyone else authorized to receive it.

Early in August Raymond Johnson called at the Society. Charlie, Raymond said, had divided his accumulated savings among his relatives some time before his death.

"When you go, Charlie," Raymond had reminded him, "you may have some salary coming."

"If I do," Charlie had answered, "tell them at the Society to buy American flags with it."

That is what Raymond Johnson had come to tell us. And that is why, in coming months, we shall look with more than ordinary reverence at the flag that flies above the entrance to our building.

❡ *The Society holds its annual meeting as it nears the end of its ninety-ninth year. Hermon Dunlap Smith, President, sees in the Society the culmination of a century of devoted effort and the sure promise of a useful future.*

Ladies and Gentlemen: Within a few months the Chicago Historical Society will be one hundred years old. We shall celebrate the anniversary in ways that our director will outline, so I shall content myself with a few general observations.

Fifty years ago, when the Society celebrated its semicentennial, Franklin H. Head, one of my predecessors in this office, remarked: "The list of men and women who have been officers and members of the Historical Society is a notable one, and embraces a goodly proportion of the men who are credited with being the makers of Chicago." The last fifty years have only emphasized the truth of that assertion. Without the earnest efforts of these men and women, without their generosity, the Society could never have survived its many trials and troubles.

Certain names stand out in the most cursory review of the Society's history: the Reverend William Barry, founder and builder of its first great collection; Henry D. Gilpin, Philadelphia scholar and philanthropist, whose bequest undoubtedly led to the revival after the Great Fire of 1871 and the lesser fire three years later; Edward G. Mason, who, almost literally, built the massive structure at Dearborn and Ontario streets which the Society occupied from 1896 to 1932; Charles B. Pike, to whom we owe our present building and a good share of our financial stability; Eugene R. Pike and Mrs. Charles B. Pike, whose bequests have enabled the Society to meet, and more than meet, the sharply rising costs of the last ten years; and Mrs. Joseph M. Cudahy, whose munificence has assured the Society's future.

Not to acknowledge our deep debt to these former officers and members would be to invite a charge of ingratitude, yet to single out a few for mention is unfair. For there have been thousands in the Society's history whose contributions have been as great, according to their means, as those whom I have named, and perhaps, at critical times, as important to the institution. The Society's very existence has depended, and still depends, upon the generosity of its members and friends. So far this year, for example, the Society has accepted gifts of museum objects and books from 151 donors, and the number would have been much larger had we been able, in good conscience, to take all that was offered. To each and every contributor, whether the contribution be in the form of a rare historical print, a book needed by the library, an annual membership, or a bequest of $100,000, I express our collective gratitude.

So much—and far less than it deserves—for the past. What of the future?

Consider our advantages: an excellent building, sound finances, a great historical collection, a knowledge of the techniques of putting that collection to use. We intend to do better everything we are doing: to present our exhibits more dramatically, more meaningfully, than ever; to attract more and more schoolchildren to our building and send them away with more in their heads than they had when they came; to enrich an already distinguished library and make its resources more usable. We also intend to do certain things that we are not now doing: to revive the program of scholarly publications that was once one of the Society's strong features; to create popular publications for a wide audience; to record, for posterity, the personal experiences of Chicagoans who have contributed in significant ways to the making of city, state, and nation. In a word, we intend not only to maintain this institution as an important cultural agency of more than local influence, but also to enlarge its usefulness to the limit of our means. If we were to do less, we would not be keeping faith with those who have made the Society what it is.

The world of 1956 is a far different place from the world of 1856. Over the years, the Chicago Historical Society has adapted itself to change, and, if I may use the word without raising a philosophical question, progress. I am confident that it will meet with equal success the challenge of the future.

⟨ *THE SOURCES. Most of the contemporary materials which constitute the text of this history come from the Society's own archives: the minute books of its Board of Trustees and Executive Committee, its annual reports, its correspondence files, its scrapbooks of notices and invitations, and, at the end, its quarterly publication,* Chicago History. *William Corkran's descriptions of Chicago and the Chicago Historical Society are from a long manuscript entitled, "A Glance at the History of Illinois, Accompanied by the Early History of Chicago," which Corkran wrote soon after the fire of 1871. The manuscript is in the Society's library.*

Contemporary newspapers have been drawn upon for accounts of the Society's activities, and for paragraphs reflecting the flavor of the times.

While the materials used here are not always explicitly described, it is believed that the reader will have little difficulty in identifying them.

⟨ *THE ILLUSTRATIONS. With four exceptions, the originals of the illustrations used in this book are in the Society's collections. The photograph of the opening of the Society's building, November 12, 1932 was supplied by the Chicago* Tribune; *the picture of Sally Rand by United Press Newspictures; "Gabby" Hartnett by the Chicago* Daily News; *and the War of 1812 Room, November 14, 1954, by the Chicago* Tribune. *For these photographs, all of which are reproduced between pages 200 and 201, and the right to publish them the Society is most grateful.*

Set in Linotype Janson

Design, composition, printing and binding by Rand McNally & Company

PRINTED IN U.S.A.